Know Better, Do Better

TEACHING THE FOUNDATIONS SO EVERY CHILD CAN READ

David Liben and Meredith Liben

1400 Centrepark Blvd, Suite 1000
West Palm Beach, FL 33401
717-845-6300

email: pub@learningsciences.com
learningsciences.com

Printed in the United States of America

21 20 19 18 17 1 2 3 4 5 6

Publisher's Cataloging-in-Publication Data
provided by Five Rainbows Cataloging Services

Names: Liben, Meredith, author. | Liben, David, author.
Title: Know better, do better : teaching the foundations so every child can read / Meredith Liben, David Liben.
Description: West Palm Beach, FL : Learning Sciences, 2019.
Identifiers: ISBN 978-1-943920-69-3 (paperback)
Subjects: LCSH: Literacy. | Literacy--Study and teaching. | Language arts. | Effective teaching. | Education. | BISAC: LANGUAGE ARTS & DISCIPLINES / Literacy. | EDUCATION / Teaching Methods & Materials / Language Arts. | EDUCATION / Professional Development. | EDUCATION / Aims & Objectives.
Classification: LCC LB1050 .L53 2019 (print) | LCC LB1050 (ebook) | DDC 372.4--dc23.

Table of Contents

Acknowledgements

So many streams feed into the river of this book. First, to name and thank our primary early reading mentors, to whom we owe debts for generosities we try daily to repay through our work: Chuck Perfetti, Tim Rasinski, Marilyn Adams, Linnea Ehri, Tim Shanahan, Freddy Hiebert, Louisa Moats, David Page, Deb Glaser, and Gwen Stephens.

We've gained insights and encouragement from numerous colleagues, and quite a few of them added responding to these chapters to their hefty workloads. Chief among them are Lorraine Griffith, Francie Alexanders, Joyce Harrison, David Page, Silas Kulkarni, Tori Filler, Carey Swanson, Alice Wiggins, Deb Glaser and Torrey Palmer. We thank you deeply.

We've had the great good luck to get paid for learning (along with working really hard). We've been more fortunate than most in this regard, thanks most recently to our affiliation with Student Achievement Partners. We wouldn't have learned enough to write this book without the opportunities working with SAP has provided.

Our gratitude and deep affection go to the parents, students and staff of The Family Academy. Truly the epitome of 'it takes a village'... To the parents: you trusted us with your children before we deserved it. You stayed with us, shifted quickly to "trust but verify" and always pushed us to be better for your children. We strive still to deserve your trust and the investment you made in us as educators. To our students: you showed us what a school could be when all the students love to read, and what all school communities should be. Our love to you as you continue to work to be your own best selves. To the staff – we built a great curriculum and school together. We worked and played hard. Each of you were instrumental.

Finally, to Luke and Zach, who put up with a reading-obsessed father and step-mom. You grew up alongside the Family Academy with little complaint about how often our attention focused away from you to it. You both added your unique contributions to our understanding of reading's place in a life. Long live *Narnia* and *Farmer Boy*

Introduction: A Story

On a beautiful late spring day in 1994, we rounded the corner of 113th Street and walked toward the building that housed the alternative public elementary school in Harlem we had started three years earlier. We were met by the sight of the principal from the school downstairs waving us down, and then we saw three New York City television news vans parked in front. Our first thoughts were that some terrible accident had happened with one of our staff or students.

The principal let us know that our young school's first efforts at taking the annual reading test had resulted in the lowest scores in all of New York City, and the press wanted faces and comments to go along with the story. She suggested we go around the back entrance. We did, escaping for just a moment longer the stark reality that we were radically failing our children.

We dodged the television coverage but had to confront the reality of how we were failing. We gave ourselves a year to figure it out and improve our children's outcomes or hand over the reins to better-equipped educators. The learning gathered in this book started on that sidewalk back in 1994.

"We" are David and Meredith Liben, two of the three teachers who opened the Family Academy in central Harlem in the fall of 1991. We had been successful middle and high school teachers in public and private schools, David for 15 years and Meredith for 9, before starting the Family Academy. The third founder, Christina Giammalva, had come to us as a volunteer at the junior high we started in East Harlem and stayed there with us for 3 years, becoming a teacher in the process. None of us had ever taught below fourth grade. We knew nothing about beginning reading, and for much of the first three years of the school, buoyed by the holistic approach to reading instruction known then as Whole Language, knew nothing about how ignorant we were.

The Family Academy was a regular public school, authorized and run under the auspices of Community School District 3, that we got permission to open in the fall of 1991.

The school was designed to answer a very simple question: If an urban school serving 100% students from low-income families had all the money it needed to educate its children as well as suburban children are, what should that school look like? Our answer was a school that was open and running all day and during the summer, provided on-site supports and services for children and their parents, had high-quality extracurricular offerings, and was 100% made up of students from families from the neighborhood. You can get a good sense of what we were striving for by reading *The New York Times* article about our school.[1]

None of those wraparound supports was provided by the New York City Department of Education (NYCDOE) nor were the comprehensive library, school band, swimming lessons, sports and theater programs, and other services we continued to build and improve. So money had to be raised from private sources, a task Christina gamely took on. At the time we started, there was little competition for educational philanthropy. There were no charter schools in New York, no Harlem Children's Zone, and little competition for support from any other grassroots educational reform efforts. National organizations such as Teach for America were just getting started, and it was the 1990s economic boom in New York City. We were able to raise all the money we needed to create the rich extracurricular programming and wraparound supports we had envisioned.

Parents were ecstatic to have their children in school all day in the same place where they themselves could take adult classes, meet with a social worker, get help with job applications, and take advantage of myriad other services. Because of the small size of the school (two classes per grade and growing just one grade bigger each year), everyone knew everyone. It was in so many respects an ideal environment. We could pay attention to the social and emotional needs, not only of students but also of their parents, and we were doing it in a close-knit community under immediate local control. The Family Academy had everything many reformers have advocated for decades, ingredients we still believe in deeply.[2]

But we had the lowest reading scores in the city of New York the year our initial class of second-grade students[3] took the citywide reading test.

Why?

A good short answer would be that the three teachers who started the school knew nothing about beginning reading. This would be true. A closely related answer would be that even if everything else is done beautifully if you don't have the right curriculum you won't have academic success. The Family

---

[1] For the article in *The New York Times* that gives a comprehensive look at the design and goals of the Family Academy: https://www.nytimes.com/1994/01/26/us/school-public-school-harlem-that-takes-time-trouble-be-family.html.

[2] See James Comer's *School Power* (1995), in particular, for a summary of the work that influenced our thinking about creating a full-service school for families.

[3] The year 1994 was the last one New York City tested second-grade students in reading and math. That meant our first group of students were the only children in the school to take the test two years running because the testing shifted to begin at third grade the same year they became third-grade students.

Academy was a dramatic example of this. But it was not an isolated phenomenon. A recent report from the Brown Center on Education analyzing 2018 National Assessment of Education Progress (NAEP) data show that the median (50th percentile) scores of children of color and children from low-income families fall between the 10th and 25th percentile scores of white and more affluent children.[4] Sadly, this has been true since a similar comparison was made back in 1996. The major reason for these discrepant results is the same reason we got the lowest reading scores in New York City back in 1994. The instructional approach we used to teach our children how to read, very similar to approaches in place in many schools today, wasn't based on any scientific evidence at all. That proves itself in our collective failure to teach too many children to read. This particularly impacts children who most need their learning accelerated by the schools they attend and the teachers who love and care for them.

Even if everything else is done beautifully if you don't have the right curriculum you won't have academic success.

Tipping our hand here—this whole book is about teaching children what they need to learn about reading on time so almost no one needs intervention. It's our goal that every child in every elementary school in America can read fluently by the end of second grade. This book explains how to make that happen—for all children in all classrooms. They get to play with sounds and the sounds letters make in kindergarten. They get to decode—learn the patterns of the English language—in first grade and come to recognize those patterns automatically and quickly—to rapidly name them. And then in second grade, they learn to read multisyllabic words and grade-level text of all sorts fluently. They do all this while getting read to multiple times a day in school so they fully know the beauty, knowledge, and wonders available to them between the pages of a book, even books they can't yet read for themselves. Then all children can unlock knowledge for themselves all the rest of their lives. That's what we're striving for. Along the way, we hope to show that a research-based reading program is most effective for *all* students. A good one will support teachers in integrating lots of fun and intellect into the rich learning.

So, in this book, we'll teach you what the research clearly points to. The good news is the research findings are consistent and clear. Yet much reading instruction is fuzzy and doesn't acknowledge those findings. Many educators are still recommending and following practices that match their training, without realizing these practices are problematic for vulnerable

[4] This is the link to the Brown Center report of the 2018 NAEP results: https://www.brookings.edu/research/2018-brown-center-report-on-american-education-trends-in-naep-math-reading-and-civics-scores/.

groups of children. And they persist in doing so even though many of their children aren't learning how to read. We'll explain what the right instructional approaches are, why they are much better for all children, and why it has been so hard for teachers and schools to embrace them. We'll share some stories that we hope will bust myths about foundational skills mastery being dreary for young students and their teachers.

We'll look at each of the elements of a research-based beginning reading (foundational skills) program. For each, we will address what it is and how it should and shouldn't be taught. We'll reference the startlingly abundant research behind why each is essential and how best to teach it.

Along the way, you'll see the changes we made at the Family Academy, how and why they worked so well, and how you can make the same changes in your school or community. We'll also share lessons learned and resources developed from the other work we've done around the United States. In the last part of the book, contained in an appendix, we'll take a close look at some core English Language Arts (ELA) programs that get it right and how you can get more information for each.

Spoiler alert! The Family Academy test scores rose to be the highest of any non-gifted school in Harlem. Part of the story of how we did that runs through these chapters, and our work at the Family Academy forms the core of who we are as educators. David was the principal of the school for the first decade. Over the course of that same period, Meredith taught kindergarten, then second grade and fifth grade before becoming the director of the Family Academy middle school.

As a result of our dramatic turnaround in reading results, the school and our work came to the attention of the New York City Education Chancellor, who sent a young man doing pro bono consulting work for the NYCDOE to study what we had done in developing our students to be such robust readers. That young man was David Coleman, one of the primary architects of the college and career ready standards movement. Since then, we've worked on and off with David. When he was chosen by the National Governors Association and the Council of Chief State School Officers to be one of the three writers of the ELA standards, he reached out to the two of us to support that work. David (Liben) synthesized the research behind the ELA standards that is captured in Appendix A,[5] and Meredith ran the two research projects that determined what text complexity meant and what levels were valid for each grade band. That body of research has underpinned all the college and career readiness standards in place across the United States today.

Who is this book for? For anyone concerned about the poor reading results of America's children but primarily for teachers: early career teachers, those

[5] Appendix A: http://www.corestandards.org/assets/Appendix_A.pdf.

in preservice, or teachers who are dissatisfied with how their students are reading. We wanted parents to be able to read this book and understand the ideas, too, so they can be educated advocates for their children. Because we wanted the concepts and research we're discussing to be accessible, we did our best to keep educational jargon out and stories and clear prose in. We also made the book somewhat interactive by posing questions and ideas to reflect on a few times in each chapter. It is your choice, of course, whether you do those or not, and if you prefer, you can interact directly with us via our website, Reading Done Right. In fact, we hope you will!

Why write this book now? Primarily because we can't stand the fact that not every child in this country learns to read in early elementary school. Children need to learn on time so they can reap all the benefits reading yields ever after. Nearly every child can learn to read. Too many don't, and far more not well enough for future academic and career success. Nonreaders and weak readers can't access the ideas, skills, and knowledge they need to be college and career ready, to engage civilly, and to have the life options they deserve.

Educational outcomes for children who initially struggle to learn to read don't have to stay low. If we follow the research into good literacy practices and use instructional materials tightly aligned with those practices, they won't. Our hope for this book is very simple: more teachers and schools will start to use the right approaches for beginning reading, and children will benefit.

Chapter One

Letter Recognition and Alphabetic Knowledge

This is Meredith's story. Ella impatiently motioned for me to move out of her way. "I can't see how to make the 'B,'" she said. "It's on the wall over there, above the door, but I can't see it with you in the way." She gestured at the alphabet chart running across the side wall of the classroom.

I moved as asked. Ella studied the alphabet chart briefly, located the card with the banana and 'B_b' on it near the "edge" of the strip as she remembered, and proceeded to write 'b' accurately on her paper (Figure 1).

FIGURE 1. Photograph of a banana used in an alphabet chart.

Ella was in kindergarten and didn't yet have solid alphabetic knowledge. She hadn't had a chance to play with, manipulate, and memorize the shapes of the letters of the English alphabet well enough to write them without a model. By mid-March, the time I was observing her class, she had learned the names of most of the letters and was starting to identify the sounds each letter made, but she couldn't always match the name of a letter to its shape.

It had taken her almost a minute to move me out of her way, locate the 'B' on the chart, and remember how to write it accurately. Meanwhile, the teacher and her classmates had moved on to a whole other section of the lesson. Ella was an intelligent child; what was missing and slowing her down was a knowledge gap because of her history, not any learning disability or intrinsic problem. She was hampered by experiences she hadn't had that most of her classmates had. Whenever the class was discussing and working with phonic patterns and were mapping sounds onto an increasing number of letters and forming words, Ella had to do extra steps *every* time to get to where other children were starting. Because Ella was so resourceful, her teacher had not realized her gaps and the toll they were taking until I chanced to be in her way, observed what was happening, and alerted her teacher to what Ella needed to quickly learn to catch up.

What exactly are alphabetic knowledge and letter recognition?

We bet you have a pretty good idea already! Before you go on, write brief working definitions in the space below and then check your definitions against ours.

Letter Recognition:

Alphabetic Knowledge:

Here are our working definitions.

Letter recognition is a subset of alphabetic knowledge. As its name implies, it is the ability to recognize and identify each letter of the alphabet by name in both its upper- and lowercase forms.

Alphabetic knowledge is the ability to recognize every letter of the alphabet in both upper- and lowercase forms, match the 26 names of the English alphabet letters to those forms, and then know the primary sounds each letter makes. Letters in English make sounds other than their names. Think, for example, about the two sounds 'C' makes (/k/ and /s/).

Are These Basic Skills Important in the Scheme of Things? A Story

This knowledge is the building block for reading the English language. It's so simple and straightforward, so loaded with common sense, that it's sometimes in danger of being skipped over in favor of going straight to the sounds those letters make. But these basic skills are essential. Research is clear that "the prerequisites for learning to decode are **letter recognition**, **letter-sound knowledge**, and phonemic awareness" [emphasis added] (Adams, 2011). A recently published study correlates kindergarteners' letter naming ability with *tenth-grade* reading comprehension ability (Stanley, Petscher, & Catts, 2017). Let's take this stunning finding back to Ella. She couldn't write 'B' without looking, which meant she spent extra time laboring over letter formation. But that also means she couldn't visualize 'B' and 'b' in her mind. It's not very likely 'B' was her only troublesome letter. Ella would be slow to recognize individual letters in print and then would have to recall what sounds were associated with each letter. This would play out during reading lessons, while doing individual work, or in any literacy activity. Slow letter recognition means words are worked out more slowly. Once Ella did all the work to recognize a word, she had to integrate that with all the other words (each labored over in turn) to read a sentence. You can see that all of Ella's working memory and problem-solving capacity was getting taken up by the laborious task of connecting her new learning to the most basic starting point, letter recognition, writing words letter by letter. Smart and resourceful as she was, she couldn't spare much thinking power for actually processing the meaning of words she was writing. If her slow letter recognition wasn't spotted and dealt with, the domino effect on her reading clearly would have damaging long-term effects. That's what this research has so clearly shown.

In short, letter recognition and alphabetic knowledge are important. They are essential building blocks in learning to read and critically important in service to that goal. They are straightforward elements of the foundational skills package, as are concepts of print, the subject of the next chapter.

Exactly Why Are They Important?

They Offer a Common Language

Letter name knowledge allows for a common language when talking about letter sounds/phonemic awareness, decoding, and spelling. Letters are really abstract. They're just symbols in two dimensions. They need to be discussed and thought about, played with and manipulated a lot before they start to make sense for young children. If everyone in the group knows the names of each of the letters, it allows the class to have a shared conversation about letters and what they do. So knowing the names of the symbols that represent sounds in written English allows for a common literacy vocabulary to be built in a classroom.

Letter Names Allow Us to Study Them and Share Insights

Just as students learn that circles are a common kind of shape that share features (no corners, round) or cats are a kind of animal that shares common features (whiskers, pointy ears), so too they learn that the /m/ sound is represented by the symbol 'M' and is named "em." Then they know what to pay attention to when we're discussing a word or sound that involves 'M.' They can see that 'M' can be represented in uppercase ('M') and in a lowercase form that looks somewhat different ('m'). Then they need to learn that some letters look *really* different in upper- and lowercase, as in the case of the symbols for 'G' and lowercase 'g' (or sometimes '*g*'). All those different forms of 'G' still have the same name.

Letter Names Ground Us until Our Letter Knowledge Is Cemented in Our Minds

The names of the letters build connections between all the different ways you know letters in your brain until those connections become automatic and disappear into the background to do their seemingly magical work. You will start to distinguish and have a picture of an 'M' when you sing the alphabet song, instead of just sliding through it fast, as "LMNO." You'll notice 'M's and 'm's (and all your learned letters) when you see them on the pages of books read to you or on street and store signs when you're out in the world. Your brain will remember 'M' for you forever so you can always and automatically retrieve and build on what you know about it as you move on to all the other aspects of becoming a reader.

Letter Awareness Is a Step toward Word Awareness

Being aware of letters makes children more aware of printed words because they are made up of groups of letters. Because all words are built from individual letters and the sounds they represent coming together in patterned ways, recognizing the letters in our alphabet is a critical component to reading.

Letter names bridge upper- and lowercase forms of letters and let children know they stand for the same thing.

Automatic Recognition

Being able to name letters rapidly (rapid naming) is a crucial component of decoding. Our brains are hard-wired to recognize physical objects and name them although we vary in how quick we are about it, but learning to recognize and name abstract symbols (letters) is not natural and must be taught and practiced. Some children need much more time practicing this than others will. That's because people vary in how quick or slow they are at rapidly identifying and naming objects. But practice can improve outcomes. Think about eye–hand coordination, another trait thought to be fixed. Some people have naturally better eye–hand coordination than others, creating a continuum of abilities for such activities as sewing or playing baseball. If you sew, for example, and want to get better at threading a needle, you can practice threading needles and get better at the task. It's the same with practicing letter recognition and naming. You might not have natural rapidity, but letter naming, in particular, can be improved through practice. The amount of practice it takes to become automatic with any skill, including letter naming, will vary widely from child to child.

Sound Sensitivity

Many (but not all) letters have a sound correspondence to their names ('A,' 'B,' 'C,' 'D,' 'E,' 'G,' 'I,' 'J,' 'K,' 'O,' 'P,' 'T,' 'U,' 'V,' and 'Z'), meaning their name begins with or sounds just like the dominant sound that letter makes in words. So learning the names of letters helps develop phonemic sensitivity (the ability to identify clearly) at the phoneme level. This can ease the transition to focusing on the sounds graphemes (letters) make that are at the heart of phonics instruction. An important note, however: this is not true for all letters. Paying attention to the connection between a letter's name and the phoneme it is used to represent can help you track students' confusion. When, for example, they begin writing, if they're using a 'd' for the /w/ sound, that may have everything to do with the name of the 'W' ("double 'u'"!). Being aware of this distinction between the name and the primary sound can help you pay close attention to this nuance when teaching. It may also help you figure out what those fertile brains are thinking!

So, alphabetic knowledge, knowing letter shapes, each letter name, and the sounds each letter can make, is critical. It is blessedly easy to teach, and the good news is that this is easy and playful work for nearly all children. It is quick and simple to acquire for most children, but that doesn't mean it's not an important ingredient to attend to.

Children need to be comfortable recognizing and naming the 52 letter shapes (26 uppercase and 26 lowercase letters). If they can recognize and name them rapidly, that is a very good sign for their reading progress. *Many* children come into kindergarten with this knowledge from home or preschool, so much so that kindergarten teachers often presume its presence and don't always check for this knowledge. That oversight leaves children such as Ella scrambling.

How Do You Teach It?

Most children love familiarity and repetition, and we generally enjoy doing things we're good at. So we don't have to worry overmuch about children with letter knowledge losing interest while we're working whole class to make sure all the children gain mastery. Some alphabet activities just make sense to do whole class whereas many other activities can be done in small groups, so children who need more practice opportunities get what they need to help them move forward.

Whole-Class Songs and Activities

The Alphabet Song. Your students will happily sing the alphabet song and will be interested in expanding their knowledge of the alphabet through it. You can:

- ask students to dissect the song elements by focusing on it letter by letter while looking at the visual of an alphabet chart.
- pick students to stand up and take turns pointing quickly at each letter to guide their fellow students in looking at each as they sing its name. Use a fancy pointer to create a festive and fun atmosphere.
- engage everyone. Give each child a letter or two to hold and have each one wave or lift it in turn when it is named in the song as the children sing it slowly.
- laugh together over the "LMNO" blending that we have all done and challenge the class to find those separate letters in the alphabet chart.

Free games for recognizing and naming letters and for learning the sounds each letter makes that are appropriate for whole-class activities abound and can be found with simple internet searches. Most of them, like the alphabet song, are geared to preschool, which is when this set of skills is most appropriately mastered.

Alphabet Books

Read high-quality alphabet books regularly as part of your kindergarten read-aloud program. Some of the most beloved picture books of all time are alphabet books. There are many gorgeous alphabet books students will request repeatedly. Some links to "best of" lists for alphabet books are included in the resources at the end of this chapter.

Because you will probably have some students who have alphabetic knowledge and some who don't, you'll want to be able to provide different experiences via small groups to give all children the experiences they need.

Be cautious when alphabet books are connected to sounds, however. If the goal is letter recognition, this work can be done in many ways, but often authors inadvertently use non-examples when connecting letter recognition to letter sounds (think "'X' is for xylophone" but also "'O' is for oven").

Small-Group Activities

There are myriad ways to make sure students learn to recognize and write letters. Cycle as many of these teaching processes through your classroom as possible. Children who have not mastered letter recognition and do not have full alphabetic knowledge of the most common representations of sounds that individual letters stand for should be systematically provided with these learning opportunities until they demonstrate mastery. All children should have access to as many of the following manipulatives as possible and be taught how to play with them to maximize their learning: alphabet blocks, books, songs, refrigerator magnets, charts, desk charts, wall charts, coloring sheets, handwriting practice with letters, digital tools, and the encouragement and instruction to write what they want to say using their letter and alphabetic knowledge to spell their words—using "inventive" or "temporary" spelling patterns.

It is vital to know where your students (or your own child) are with alphabetic knowledge and to address any gaps so all children have the necessary knowledge they need to move forward with reading. Make sure you assess and keep track of where each child is in moving toward solid letter recognition and naming and the progress each has made in learning the dominant sound for each letter.

How Do You Assess Letter Recognition and Alphabetic Knowledge?

The two parts of alphabetic knowledge need to be assessed separately.

1. Letter naming: Children should be able to match the spoken names of each letter with both their upper- and lowercase forms. Free online assessment tools only spot check this knowledge. You need to know that *every* child knows the name of *every* letter and can recognize each letter in both cases.
2. Alphabetic knowledge: Children should use letters with increasing accuracy to spell the phonemes they identify in words. The absolutely best way to know if your students are getting more sophisticated at knowing what sounds each letter makes is through regularly analyzing their inventive spelling.

Early on, they might appropriately use letter names as stand-ins for the sounds words make, for example, 'DA' (= day), 'JRF' (= giraffe), or 'R' (= are). These young children are brilliant! They are demonstrating the understanding that letters are integrated into words and that written words represent spoken words. They are applying that understanding in rational, patterned ways. Even though there is more to it than those beautiful one-to-one correspondences they are creating, these children are abstracting important knowledge and demonstrating what they know.

Starting to isolate more sounds and knowing what letters make those sounds will come along when phonemic awareness and alphabetic knowledge are both activated at once, as should be increasingly the case through kindergarten. You should start to see 'SKL' (= school), 'DNSR' (= dinosaur), or 'GRL' (= girl). Short vowel sounds are much harder to identify than consonant sounds, so don't worry about missing vowels until children are working with phonic patterns such as CVC (consonant-vowel-consonant) words (e.g., cat, pop, or lit).

Once children have been taught a phonic pattern though, you should expect to see them produce those patterns accurately in their writing. This is true for whole words you've taught by sight, too. If they can't, it means they didn't learn them, and your diagnosis here should lead you to provide these children with more practice opportunities to strengthen the weak areas. That is the world of systematic phonics, *and* it touches on phonological awareness, too. We'll be providing you with lots more detail in upcoming chapters.

How Do You Provide Alphabetic Knowledge for Students with Unfinished Learning in This Area?

Letter recognition is essential for the many shared communications and common references we make to letter names in our classrooms. It's also essential to know the sounds letters make and to understand what letter someone is referring to when you're learning to read in English. Although this is a finite area of learning and very straightforward, it's important to make sure everyone has acquired these skills.

Whether our English learners come to us from a nonalphabetic language (such as Mandarin) or knowing another alphabet, they need to learn the names of the letters in the English alphabet to enable common naming conventions in their quest to learn to read and write English. This is equally true of literate monolingual English speakers who are studying another language, just in reverse. Students learning Russian or Ancient Greek need to first learn the names of the Cyrillic or Greek letters and the sounds associated with them before they can do almost anything else. But this can be done quickly and then dispensed with.

Some Final Things to Keep in Mind

This learning can and should be fun for children! Make it active. Encourage your students to use their whole body, to move to sides of the room for distinguishing 'b' from 'd' and 'p' and 'q,' or jump up in place when they recognize an uppercase letter that matches the lowercase counterpart. The sky's the limit to making this learning lively.

Uppercase letters are more distinct symbols and tend to be easier to identify and write. Many preschool programs suggest starting with them, but we didn't find any research with solid recommendations or guidance regarding the benefit to teaching one case before another or on how long to wait between teaching both cases of a letter. We recommend you simply follow the guidance of the foundational skills program you're using. English is a systematic and reliable language even if it isn't always straightforward. That's important to transmit to children at many junctures, along with the promise that system will be revealed to them as they learn it. Any good foundational skills program will help communicate that through its own systematic approach.

The motor component of forming letters—following correct letter formation and using a pencil or crayons on paper—helps build brain pathways for remembering letters. Capitalize on this practice. Say letter names clearly, provide a model of correct letter formation, and ask students to write the letters after you. Honor your students writing; it is their creation, but make sure it's legible and the letter formation is as accurate as they can manage.

Spread out the introduction to similar-looking letters ('p,' 'd,' 'b,' and 'q,' or 'm,' and 'w'), and teach the letters with clearly differentiated shapes earlier. It's also good to learn the letters early where the sound they stand for begins their names: 'B,' 'J,' 'K,' 'P,' 'T,' 'Z,' 'D,' and 'V.' Notice we separated 'B,' 'P,' and 'D' because their lowercase forms ('b,' 'p,' and 'd') are confusing to children who haven't yet grasped that the position of the letter matters nearly as much as its shape. After all, a triangle is a triangle no matter which direction it faces. But letters have to face a certain way. Talk about that directly, but don't be surprised by how frequently children mix this up at first. After that, you could teach the letters for which the sound they stand for is the second sound children will hear in their names: 'F,' 'L,' 'M,' 'N,' 'R,' 'S,' and 'X.' Then, of course, there are the *very* confusing letter names for which there's no connection between their name and the sound they stand for: 'H,' 'W,' and 'Y.' Of course, if the materials you're relying on have an order of introduction, it is fine to follow it! Just keep these factors in mind so you can point them out to the children.

Just make sure your students know the name of each letter in each form and grasp the idea that every letter has at least two shapes.

You can move faster than you think. There is research that the "Letter of the Week" approach weakens children's sound–symbol connection making by focusing *too* much on the symbol and name of each letter in isolation. Introduce two or three letters a week and keep cycling the taught letters with the newly introduced ones until everyone is confident with everything.

Letter identification and naming are in service of learning to read. They are a means, not an end in themselves. Don't overemphasize it as its own area of mastery. Contextualize letters in their roles as sound representatives and their important role as the *things* words are made of.

If you're teaching kindergarten, like Ella's teacher, or even first grade, you can't safely assume your children have alphabetic knowledge. They probably all won't, and glossing over this gap will have serious consequences for those students who don't have mastery of the alphabet. You have to be sure all your students attain mastery on your watch, meaning they're all able to identify every letter by name, recognize them in upper- and lowercase forms, and know the most common sound each letter makes. Make sure you can account for everyone's growth and mastery through the types of assessments we discussed. Otherwise, you're overlooking an important and easy-to-fix element that will stop your students from being positioned to prosper as beginning readers.

Sources for Deeper Learning and Teaching

Excellent two-page article on rapid naming a source of reading difficulty from Tufts Child Development Center

https://ase.tufts.edu/crlr/documents/FAQNamingSpeedDeficit.pdf

Good website for alphabetic activities:

Literacy for All Canada from the Edmonton (Alberta) Regional Learning Consortium

http://literacyforallinstruction.ca/alphabet-phonological-awareness/

Good resource from Arizona Department of Education with activities at the end

https://cms.azed.gov/home/GetDocumentFile?id=59397eb63217e108981dda92

Recorded video of the Alphabet Song with refrigerator magnet letters

https://www.youtube.com/watch?v=Y88p4V_BCEU

Classic alphabet books

ABC, Doctor Seuss (1960)

Chicka Chicka Boom Boom, Bill Martin (1989)

Great alphabet books for older children

Take Away the A, by Michael Escoffier (2014)

The Graphic Alphabet, David Pelletier (1996)

P is for Pterodactyl: The Worst Alphabet Book Ever, by Raj Haldar (2018)

"Best of" alphabet picture books list

https://www.joyfullythriving.com/best-alphabet-books/

Teaching alphabet knowledge to older-than-average students

https://classroom.synonym.com/teach-alphabet-adults-8077909.html

https://busyteacher.org/17917-how-to-teach-abc-to-adults-7-proven-ways.html

Free, quick online assessment tool from Reading Rockets

http://www.readingrockets.org/article/get-ready-read-screening-tool

Works Consulted

Adams, M. (1990). *Beginning to read: Thinking and learning about print.* Cambridge, MA: MIT Press.

Adams, M. (2011). The relation between alphabetic basics, word recognition, and reading. In S. J. Samuels & A. E. Farstrup (Eds.), *What research has to say about reading instruction* (pp. 4–24). Newark, DE: International Reading Association.

Cunningham, A. E., & Stanovich, K. E. (1998). The impact of print exposure on word recognition. In L. C. Ehri & J. L. Metsala (Eds.), *Word recognition in beginning literacy* (pp. 235–262). Hillsdale, NJ: Erlbaum.

Piasta, S. B., & Wagner, R. K. (2010). Learning letter names and sounds: effects of instruction, letter type, and phonological processing skill. *Journal of Experimental Child Psychology, 105*, 324–344. doi:10.1016/j.jecp.2009.12.008.

Stanley, C. T., Petscher, Y., & Catts, H. (2017). A longitudinal investigation of direct and indirect links between reading skills in kindergarten and reading comprehension in tenth grade. *Reading and Writing, 31*, 133–153. doi:10.1007/s11145-017-9777-6.

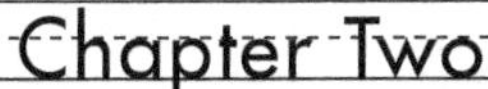

Chapter Two

Concepts of Print

Several years ago, we were visiting schools in Iowa, observing the implementation of a high-quality English Language Arts program (we'll discuss these in the appendix at the end of the book). At one wonderfully successful school, we remarked on how "into the lesson" children seemed to be in the first grade we had just observed and noted one particularly eager girl. The literacy coach told us a story about that little girl who, as we said, was noticeably *into* all the reading and language activities.

Hani was a young Somali refugee who had been resettled with her family in the district early the fall before. She'd been placed into kindergarten because she was six years old but had not had any school opportunities. She'd spent her whole life up to then in Dadaab, a huge complex of refugee camps in Kenya, where she had been born after her parents fled ethnic violence in Somalia. During her kindergarten year in Iowa, her expressive language rapidly improved (she had learned a fair amount of English in the camp in Kenya), and being social, Hani had integrated well into the class. The coach noted Hani seemed to enjoy the phonemic awareness games and activities and was successful at them. The small doses of phonics the kindergarten teacher was exposing the students to were also being snapped up with ease by this child when the words were introduced in isolation. But she was utterly unable to apply these skills whenever a book was involved. She'd be lost when the class shifted to using these newfound skills in a book.

What was going on?

Initially, her kindergarten teacher and the coach were equally at a loss and frustrated until they interviewed Hani's mom and figured out what was causing the disconnect.

It seemed Hani had never seen a book before she came to school. Although some parts of the camp had managed to set up some educational services for school-aged children, Hani had been too young to be part of anything organized. She didn't know what a book was or how the sound games she was playing at school, and even the symbols of the alphabet the teachers were showing her in cards and on the board, translated to a rectangle of cardboard and paper with letters and pictures covering every page. She didn't know that books were objects you could hold in your hands or that they were a source from which to learn things and to get great stories and ideas into your mind.

Her teacher and the literacy coach sprang into action. They had noticed, but it hadn't registered as a problem, that Hani always stared off into space during read-alouds, enjoying the oral reading but, they realized, never paying close attention to the interaction between the teacher and the book. Because they had previously felt the primary goal of reading aloud to children was to get them to enjoy books and reading, they had no systems in place to encourage children to pay attention visually, just aurally. They suspected Hani might not have connected the spoken sentences with the object the teacher held in her hands. So they made sure Hani sat where she could see the books during the several daily read-alouds, and they told her that thing was a *book* and that was where the stories and learning came from. Her teacher started to expand the types of interactions and connections she made when she read aloud, moving beyond just content wonderings to features of print. She made sure to point out the title and that it was on the cover, or front, of the book. She talked about the fact that pages turned from left to right (from the front toward the back), and sentences were read that way too, from the top of the page to the bottom. She pointed out commas and periods that told her when to catch her breath and to think about what she had just read. She showed her comic book with speech bubbles and story books with quotation marks, telling her there were different ways you can show people are talking to one another in print. She pointed out different font appearances and connected them to the letter names and sounds Hani was so good at in other parts of the day. (As a note: These practices have become common practice for the kindergartens and preschools in this district since this experience with Hani.)

They matched Hani with a reading buddy from her class, another girl who was conversant with books and loved to "play school." The two girls were encouraged to "read" books together daily and to write stories when they were working in their journals and at the writing center. They made sure that anyone reading with Hani always pointed out the book's title and what it was for, how the pages turned, how the pictures connected to what she was hearing on each page, and finally, that the sentences the reader said were represented by the words and marks on the page. And on the weekends, they sent home some of the books Hani had "read" with her buddy and encouraged her to "read" those stories to her parents and little brothers, page by page.

They said it was so simple once they figured it out. After just a couple of immersive weeks, Hani was hooked on books. We had just seen the results for ourselves in the exuberant little girl we'd noticed in our first-grade observation.

If the school administered any sort of Early Reading Inventory, it wouldn't have taken any time before Hani's lack of book awareness was noticed. In the very first kindergarten (or pre-K) assessment, children are routinely screened for print awareness. The instructional materials Hani's school was using (that we were there to observe in action) had not incorporated an Early Reading Inventory into its materials, but the publisher recommends doing so now!

If any child doesn't seem to track well when read to (and there are specific indicators to look for included in the Early Reading Inventories) or doesn't understand the concepts of print, how a book works, or, like Hani, what a book is, the school is expected to spring into action to provide the experiences that will make that clear—just as Hani's teacher and the literacy coach did for her.

Everyone in a school could participate: administrators, teachers, book-savvy peers from the class, custodians, lunchroom and office staff, upper-grade students, and parent volunteers. What a great message that would send. Nothing is more important than literacy, and nothing is more important than helping the children we need to help the most in joining in the experience with their classmates of the joys of being read to. And during the course of this joy, developing an understanding of how books work.

What Are Concepts of Print? A Story

As you've probably already inferred from the story about Hani, concepts of print, also known as print awareness, are "the basic understandings of reading" (McKenna & Stahl, 2009). The ways children acquire print awareness are:

- mainly through being read to *while* concepts of print are pointed out to them,
- by holding and reading books themselves,
- retelling books to themselves,
- playing with letters,
- playing with word and sentence formation in various forms (blocks, magnets, sentence strips, games), and
- having opportunities to try to form words and to "write" their own ideas on paper or a screen.

These things happen at home for lucky children, but they must happen in school for *all* children because it is essential that all children get these experiences, as Hani's teacher and coach so wisely recognized.

Because being aware of the concepts of print is being aware of how reading itself works, it is obvious how important it is for children to gain such awareness. The good news is that this is one of the simplest, most pleasurable aspects of literacy! That is true for adults as well as children.

How Do You Teach Concepts of Print?

It's easy and fun to teach concepts of print! You read to children in your care—a lot. While you read, you show them how the book is constructed just as you'd naturally share the pictures on each page. A great tool for this, especially if your class is large, is a document camera; the book you're reading can be magnified on a screen or whiteboard. Big Books, which are simply poster-sized versions of popular picture books, are lower-tech ways of sharing the concepts of print while you read aloud. In both cases, all the children can easily see the pictures and sentences even if they are not sitting right near you. This same effect can be created by reading aloud to students in smaller groups or by very thoroughly walking the book around your group of students while showing them the illustrations and pointing out the features of print you're talking about.

What are those features? Book features involve understanding how books are put together:

- that they have a cover and a back,
- that the cover has a title on it that tells you something about the book inside,
- that they are written by people (authors) and illustrated by artists (illustrators),
- that pages are numbered so you can keep track of where you are, and
- that their pages are read from top to bottom and left to right.

You can use your finger or another pointer to track where you're reading and to model how pages flow, which also has the benefit that you won't lose your place when you look up to listen to a student's question or idea or need to monitor behavior.

Concepts of print include the ideas that:

- words have white space around them,
- sentences begin with capital letters and end with punctuation (a period, a question mark, or an exclamation mark).
- you show children what those marks look like,
- you point out how you change your voice when you "read" one of those marks:
  - a full stop and breath for a period,
  - a rising voice at the end before you stop and take a breath for a question mark, and
  - a louder and excited voice for an exclamation mark before you take a breath between sentences.

There are other learnings going on while children are mastering concepts of print—all equally pleasurable and important. Children are learning vocabulary and gaining knowledge of how language works in books. They're seeing a variety of ways sentences work and gaining a sense of syntax. They're also learning about the structure of text itself. If the books they're exposed to are as wide ranging as they should be, they're also learning the differences between literary and informational texts, between fiction and nonfiction.

You should cement *all* this learning and demonstrate its value by letting children write books themselves and sometimes making books together as a class. Children should be encouraged to "write" their stories and ideas on paper and illustrate those stories. Even if their writing is still more scribbling than legible, they should still be encouraged to put space around their words and punctuate the way authors do in the books they've seen and heard.

The Author's Party

At the Family Academy, we hosted Author's Parties in every kindergarten classroom twice a year. The first party would be in the late fall to reinforce the concepts of print early and to cement literacy as a high value worth celebrating. In a nice two-for-the-price-of-one—because the first event's books were generally a combination of students' scribble, random letters, some invented spelling, and student dictation captured by the adults—the celebrations were also a great opportunity to teach parents how literacy developed. The books were simply file folders with pages stapled into them, complete with cover art, titles, and all the features of a book.

All children would display their favorite of the books they had constructed and would stay near it to discuss it with their admiring public. Each book had "Readers' Comments" pages bound into them (which followed the "About the Author" page). Everyone who visited that child's display and read the book would write congratulatory notes on that page. These were festive events that parents, teachers, and older siblings all looked forward to. These events were always followed by a potluck dinner eaten together in the classrooms. Staff and the other parents lavished extra attention on the children whose parents couldn't make it that afternoon.

The spring celebration put on display the developmental progress the children had made over the course of the year while again celebrating the children as authors. Through this simple, much-beloved tradition, we brought the school community together to celebrate the budding literacy of the youngest students.

Many schools have something like this; we were not unique in having Authors' Parties. But it's worth stopping to catalog just how many benefits traditions like this bring into a school community. Consider introducing the process into your setting if you possibly can.

Whenever you're reading what children have written, to risk offending, you should probably play it safe and ask your students (or your own child!) to read what they wrote to you because you sometimes won't be able to read it for yourself. Be sure to extend their print awareness by asking them (when their voices come to a stop), "Don't you need a period (or question mark or exclamation) there to mark the end of that sentence?" or "You read more words than you are pointing to on the page. Did you miss a word?" In every encounter of children's efforts, be sure to extend their understanding while always validating their efforts and creativity. By doing so, you're constantly reminding them of how joyous it is to communicate and to be communicated with in writing.

Before you go on to Phonological Awareness, the other bedrock of early literacy…

Name several ways the activities and ideas in this chapter provide opportunities for important informal diagnostic work to happen regarding children's literacy. Consider language skills, letter knowledge, and alphabetic understanding. Others?

After reading this, is there anything you would change about how you approach and teach Concepts of Print?

Sources for Deeper Learning and Teaching

A short, comprehensive resource from the Legit Literacy website.

Warning: this website is uneven in quality! This particular page is very good although some links were broken when we visited it. This is the source where we found the elegant McKenna and Stahl (2009) quote defining Concepts of Print.

https://legitliteracy.weebly.com/concepts-of-print.html. .

An excellent resource from the Texas Education Agency and hosted on Reading Rockets

This is itself a reliable source for all things reading. It outlines the kinds of activities children at home and students pre-K or kindergarten should engage in to build a strong concept and awareness of print. It includes an easy-to-apply assessment for determining how knowledgeable children are about concepts of print.

http://www.readingrockets.org /article/print-awareness-guidelines -instruction

A link to American Reading Company's Independent Reading Level Assessment overview

https://www.americanreading.com/leveling/overview/

Marilyn Adams' seminal book, *Beginning to Read* (1990)

This is not for the faint of heart. It includes a discussion of the importance of print awareness.

Works Consulted

Adams, M. J. (1990). *Beginning to read: Thinking and learning about print.* Cambridge, MA: MIT Press.

McKenna, M. C., & Stahl, K. A. D. (2009). *Assessment for reading instruction* (2nd ed.). New York, NY: Guilford.

Chapter Three

Phonological and Phonemic Awareness

If you're a kindergarten teacher or you're fortunate enough to know a five-year-old, try asking him or her what a sound is. After immersing ourselves in the research behind teaching early reading, teachers would do this with each new group of kindergarten students. Whenever we did this, we would get answers such as "when the TV is too loud," "a noise," "a siren," and "A sound is loud!" Before too long, and with more questioning, someone would offer a version of "A sound is something you can hear," and the group would generally agree. Sometimes, the group would name the idea right then and there that most things have a sound connected to them (a train has its whistle, a dog has its bark, people have their voices), an insight we would assure students was brilliant and important that we would explore later on.

When the group had thoroughly explored the idea of sounds, we would move on to ask, "What is a word?" This was usually a whole different story. The first response was often puzzled silence. Encouraged to "think harder with their brains" (a frequent admonishment at Family Academy), children would come up with, "something you say," "a thing," "what you say when you talk," "something in a book," and "what a book is made of."

We would follow these good ideas by asking the class to stop for a minute, close their eyes, and think of a word in their minds. Some typical responses would be "mother," "father," "school," "book," "TV," or a favorite food or game. Almost always, children chose something concrete. We would then pick a volunteer to stand up and say her word to the class. We would then ask if what she *said* was the same as the object or thing she named. More puzzled faces.

We'd move the conversation, always looking for the examples that would get as many laughs as possible. For example, if a student chose ice cream, we would ask him to eat what he just said: How does it taste? Did you finish it? They would, of course, all realize that was very silly and laugh more. We would then say, "OK, you can't eat what Rochelle just said, so let's write it here instead. Now for sure we can eat it, right?" This would be followed by even more laughter. We'd just shown them words can be

We'd just shown them words can be represented in print as well as heard and understood when spoken, even if neither form was edible.

represented in print as well as heard and understood when spoken, even if neither form was edible. We would say, "A word can be spoken, and a word can be written."

We would then circle back and ask, "Now what do you think a word is?" Most of the time students will offer something like, "It tells you what you're thinking." "It's not real, but it puts pictures in your brain." We end up by bringing everybody around to agree that a word is not a thing. But you can use words to tell someone about the things you are thinking. And other people can use words to tell you what things they're thinking about.

Why go through all of this trouble and take all this time, possibly over a few days of conversation? Why not just tell children what a word is? Why is a process of discovery like this followed by explicit teaching effective? Write your thoughts in the space below.

Here's our reason why:

Good foundational skills instruction needs to teach the essential skill of recognizing words accurately, automatically, and fluently, to enable reading for understanding. As essential as this is (and it is very essential), it is not enough. Foundational skills instruction in primary school is, for nearly all children, their introduction to the idea of language itself; its nature, form, and structure; its beauty; and its purpose. And how very much fun language is to think about and work with. We take every opportunity to explain what it is, how it works, its structure, and its many purposes. We create a culture of valuing language and words—of celebrating our students' explorations into the world of formal language study.

This exploration starts in the beginning with an understanding of three features of language: what words are, what work they do, and that words exist in two forms (spoken and written). The best instructional materials do this beautifully, and we will touch on our favorites in an appendix at the end of the book. If your materials don't, you'll need to create this spirit of exploration and wonder for your students yourself.

Our Early Literacy Experience: A Story

At the Family Academy, we knew our students weren't learning to read even before we got the lowest reading scores in the city. Those scores just burned the reality onto our consciousness *and* our consciences. When we started, in the fall of 1991, the Whole Language approach was all the rage. In a nutshell, the premise behind Whole Language is that in print-rich environments where students are surrounded by books and read to frequently they will naturally learn on their own to read independently. The activities privilege meaning-making over learning how to recognize words by decoding the patterns in them, assuming those skills will fall into place. Because none of us knew anything about reading research, the intuitive, natural approach made sense to us, and we adopted it wholesale. The problem was that it didn't work for our students at all.

The first catalysts for our change had happened before those test results arrived. Our second group of kindergarten students and every group who followed after were the beneficiaries. Appropriately enough, one catalyst came in the form of a book.[1] Luckily for us, *Beginning to Read* (Adams, 1990) had just been published a year before we opened the school. (Unluckily for our first class of students, we didn't discover it until they were deep in first grade.) The book lays out, clearly and thoroughly, all that was then known about how the human brain learns to read. The book has stood the test of time, with research since its publication validating and extending Adams' findings. Adams was an experimental psychologist who was commissioned by the US Department of Education to settle the "reading wars" that raged starting in the mid-1980s between Whole Language and systematic phonics (more about this in chapter 4).

> *Phonological awareness—the awareness that spoken language is composed of units such as sounds, syllables, and words, which can be identified and manipulated—is considered by many the single greatest predictor of success in early reading.*

Beginning to Read and lots of later research show with *overwhelming* evidence that phonological awareness—the awareness that spoken language is composed of units such as sounds, syllables, and words, which can be identified and manipulated—is considered by many the single greatest

[1] The other early catalyst was a teacher, Gwen Stephens, who joined us in our second year. Gwen had knowledge and training in foundational reading and was skeptical of the Whole Language approach we junior high teacher-founders were blindly following. We started to watch what Gwen was doing and how effective it was.

predictor of success in early reading. This makes complete sense because a word is a series of sounds, called phonemes, ordered to create a unit of meaning, the word. Without understanding this basic idea, the whole enterprise of decoding words in print into something a reader understands is threatened. For this reason, we recommend beginning early to engage children in discussions and activities to help them understand what a word is and that it can be spoken or written. It is important that this happens right away in kindergarten, preschool settings, and at home as soon as children are seeing books and hearing words.

Quick Clarifications and Background

The difference between phonemic and phonological awareness is confusing. It doesn't help that researchers often use them interchangeably!

Here are our working definitions of the two types of awareness:

- Phonological Awareness: This is the universe of sounds, mostly sounds intentionally made by humans. But some programs, like Adams' practical book of games and activities we'll discuss later, start with getting children good at discriminating environmental sounds as a warm-up to being able to focus on the sounds associated with speech. It covers the ideas that spoken words are composed of units of sound that can be identified and manipulated. These units include whole words, larger units such as syllables, and then the individual sounds in words, which are phonemes.
- Phonemic Awareness: This is focused exclusively on these smallest units of sound in words: phonemes. The listening for, identification of, manipulating and playing with speech sounds help create the awareness of phonemes that combine to make words. By "playing with speech sounds," we mean blending, segmenting, deleting, and transposing (changing or swapping out sounds for other possibilities) sounds. These game-like activities are actually terribly important for reading success.

So phonological awareness is the big tent under which all of these skills relating to attending to and manipulating units of sound live. Phonemic awareness is a specific type of phonological awareness relating only to the individual speech sounds that make up words. A rectangle and a square share the same relationship—all squares are rectangles, but not all rectangles are squares. All of phonemic awareness is part of phonological awareness, but not all phonological awareness is phonemic awareness.

Both phonemic awareness and phonological awareness are developed and sharpened through active involvement of ears and mouths, no letters. When we show you the games and activities, you'll see they could be done

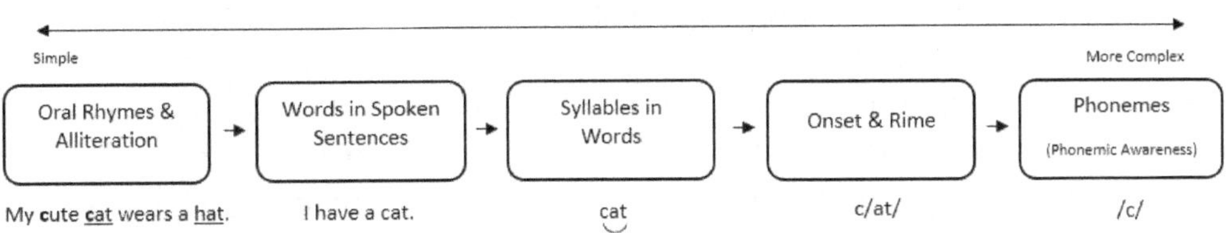

FIGURE 1. From *Achieve the Core*. Reproduced under a Creative Commons Public Domain Dedication License.

"with the lights out" or with eyes closed (and sometimes are). Rarely will you need props or preparation. How often can you say that? In fact, phonemic and phonological awareness skill building can initially be separate from formal work with the alphabet, whether learning letter names or practicing writing letters. Different parts of the brain are at work, and different skills are being developed. Students can be working on phonemic awareness skills that are far beyond the phonics they are initially learning. For example, they can *hear and say* the /oi/ sound as in as in *boil* or *boy* way before they would be seeing that as a decoding pattern. We can ask children to "Say 'boy.' Tell me the sounds in boy: /b/ /oi/."[2] And, of course, we can work on rhyming words with boy, toy, annoy, and soy, all orally.

Children will learn what a word is and gradually add to their awareness and knowledge of other elements of spoken knowledge. A research-based phonological awareness curriculum will help you do this work. This chapter will help you understand phonological awareness as it moves from listening to and identifying larger basic units to the smallest: sentences to words, words into syllables, and then words into onsets and rimes,[3] and finally the study of the phoneme itself. That learning is done with games that develop skills for students with individual phonemes that will build their phonemic awareness.

The chart below (Figure 1) may help you see this same idea in a visual form.

All of this is in keeping with the idea that a good foundational skills program should teach children about language and how it works. Some of the newer programs do this almost exclusively with games and hands-on

---

[2] Throughout the book, when we refer to the sound a letter (or cluster of letters) makes, we'll put it in slashes (/oi/). When we refer to letters by name, we'll place them in quotes 'oi.'

[3] Quick refresher on onsets and rimes: Onsets are any consonant sounds that come before the vowel in a syllable; the vowel and any consonant sounds that follow in that syllable are the rime.

activities, but there are many solid foundational skills programs that don't include fun games. You could add games of your own similar to the ones we suggest here. We'll list what we consider to be the best of these programs in the appendix. Remember, this work can be just as powerful in preschool as well as kindergarten and can be done or reinforced at home, too.

Spoken language doesn't signify much or convey meaning if the person on the receiving end isn't in the habit of listening carefully. For this reason, making sure children develop good listening discrimination has to happen even earlier. Let's begin then with listening skills, essential to phonological awareness and not a bad way to start the year in pre-K or kindergarten.

These activities are all games. Most of them can be done in 5–15 minutes with every student getting multiple opportunities. Given their importance and how quick and fun they are, they should be done more than once a day. Once you feel the class has pretty much mastered a given skill, you'll move on to the next although activities can and should be revisited throughout the year. You'll find students often resist "retiring" a game because they're all fun. It's important to spend as much time as possible in pre-K and kindergarten mastering the early levels of phonemic awareness, but many teachers have found reviewing early in first grade to be helpful. The research is clear that students need phonemic awareness to become solid readers, so you need to provide it for students until they demonstrate mastery, even if that is well into second grade. *It is not an option to skip or shortchange phonemic awareness! Children without mastery of it will inevitably struggle.* If phonemic awareness does need to be addressed in first or even second grade, it is important that it be done alongside beginning phonics, not as a precursor. First- and second-grade students can handle both types of learning together, and direct phonics instruction can't, and doesn't need to, wait on mastery of phonemic awareness. In fact, these two components of foundational skills reinforce each other.

It is not an option to skip or shortchange phonemic awareness! Children without mastery of it will inevitably struggle.

We will be giving some examples of games for each element of phonological awareness (sentence, word, syllable, onset and rime, phoneme), but these are examples only, designed to give you a flavor of these type of activities; the appendix contains references to numerous free or inexpensive sources for more of these types of activities. You will see that these games are ideal for developing expressive language and vocabulary as well, and therefore, students should be encouraged at first and then expected to answer in complete sentences when that works for the activity you're doing with them. As a rule, you should try to allow for as many students as possible to have meaningful practice with phonological or phonemic awareness activities. To do this, rather than calling on one student with a raised hand, try calling on students randomly (or based on who you know would profit most from the exercise), using whole-class choral responses, asking students to whisper to a partner first or themselves before sharing with the whole class. All of these games can be done with the whole class or in small groups, with small groups being ideal for work with students needing more time and attention.

Phonological Awareness: Listening[4]

Foundational skills instruction requires, at every level, listening that meets what we've dubbed the "Three A's": [children being] alert, active, and analytical. For young children (and a lot of us nonchildren), games are by far the best way to develop the Three A's of listening. Games allow for lots of practice and learning to happen without noticing.

What follows are examples of some of these types of games. Don't skip this section because you aren't actively teaching or parenting young children! The "whys" are baked into the activity descriptions.

Sounds and Listening Games

1. *Listening to Sounds*: The simplest of all games is simply to ask students to be silent, close their eyes, and listen to the sounds they hear. This can be done anywhere you and your children find yourselves because sounds are everywhere. After doing it once and getting your students to report what they heard, you can quickly repeat the experience to see if students hear the same sounds as the first time. Change the times of day and locations for comparisons and novelty and to build students' ability to really listen, *hear*, and describe in words the sounds flowing into their ears. They'll get better and better at this, and it is a skill that will serve them well with what comes a little later with reading.

Important building blocks to enrich this basic game are asking students to:

- rate the sound by volume of the sound by keeping their eyes closed and holding up fingers, 0–5 (which also serves two other valuable purposes:

[4] We are once again especially indebted to Marilyn Adams, this time for her book, *Phonemic Awareness in Young Children*, which is a treasure chest of the type of activities we are presenting here in limited numbers and as examples. We have recommended this book to hundreds of teachers throughout the country. None has been disappointed. It's worth noting that Adams includes lots of global phonological awareness games in spite of her confining title! As we said, even the researchers get sloppy with their language sometimes!

a quick way to spot children who may have hearing problems worth checking out *and* a good introduction to understanding "volume," a powerful academic word),

- compare and discuss the activity done with eyes open versus closed,
- do it at home and compare sounds at home versus sounds at school,
- do it on field trips to hear novel sounds, and
- listen for the *order* the sounds came in and working together as a group to report that accurately and completely.

2. *Sequence of Sounds*: Students close their eyes while teachers (or a chosen classmate) make two or three common sounds (closing a door, coughing, clapping, dropping an object, etc.). Students are then asked to identify each sound and agree on the sequence. You can expand on this by doing a specific sequence of sounds and then repeating by adding a new one or omitting a sound from the first sequence and asking students what changed. You can also add more sounds to the sequence to make it more challenging.

The following are basic activities that will build up to understanding that a word is made up of sounds in a specific sequence. That knowledge is essential to phonological awareness as well as to understanding what a word is and being able to tease apart its separate sounds. When students start to decode (read) using learned phonics patterns, they will come to understand that the sounds letters and groups of letters make in a word often depend upon what precedes or follows them in that word. That is going to come later, but we want you to see what is coming and the connections between parts of foundational skills.

3. *Listening for What Doesn't Make Sense*: Kids love this, especially when you inject humor. It is simply taking any text that you have read to students (or students know well) and changing it around. You can use anything you know is well known to all: songs, poems, or stories. Perhaps you could use "Twinkle, twinkle little (bar, car, moose, etc.)" in place of "star." If you are not sure that all of your students know a particular text, song, or poem, it's better to use something you read or sing regularly in class to ensure the children all know the text so all can participate. In that case, you can reread some pages correctly and then make a silly and obvious change. From *Where the Wild Things Are*, after the book has been read lots and discussed, swap

[5] From the original: "And when he came to the place where the wild things are they roared their terrible roars and gnashed their terrible teeth and rolled their terrible eyes and showed their terrible claws." Sendak, M., & Schickele, P. (1963). *Where the wild things are*. Weston, CT: Weston Woods.

out the text as written by inventing changes such as "they roared their terrible *whispers* and *mashed* their terrible *potatoes* and rolled their terrible *bellies*."[5]

Another way to integrate this is to do the same thing with nonfiction. The purpose here is not so much for humor but to help cement important information. From Gail Gibbons' *Bats*, instead of "A bat sends out a rapid beeping sound too high pitched for people to hear," read it as "A bat sends out a rapid beeping sound which can hurt people's ears," and then stop, help children trace the difference, and then discuss the true versus misleading statements.

Many of these activities can and should be repeated throughout the year. But this one is especially useful because it's teaching sophisticated listening *comprehension* as much as it is careful listening habits.

These are just sample activities to give you a sense of what to gather yourself. You can find or invent many more of these kinds of activities.

Another important listening skill is for children to be able to hear and make rhymes. This means they're really hearing what sounds stay the same and what sounds change inside words. Some children may already be good at rhyming, but others may need lots of practice before they start to hear the distinct sounds and patterns.

Rhyming Games

4. *Rhyming Name Games*: This gets silly quickly, which makes it especially fun for young children. Start with common classroom or household objects and play with putting new first sounds onto the word. For example, start with "wall" and model transforming it until children catch on. "Wall" can become "Paul," "mall," "tall," and "ball" in no time. There are endless variations: children's names, foods, animals, or words from the titles of beloved books are but a few.

5. *Read Rhyming Books*: There are *many* of these, and the appendix lists books and sites for rhyming activities. While you're reading rhyming books, it's good to stop and ask students to tell you the words that rhyme. Some teachers have extended this by asking students to find rhymes for other words in the book or to make nonsense words (made up words) that rhyme with the original rhymes.

6. *Rhyming and Moving*: Also a very simple game. You read pairs of words. If they rhyme children stand up and do a designated move: hop, stretch, jump, dance, whatever you can handle in your setting.

> Full-body responses aid learning, and of course, they're fun. They also give everybody a chance to move frequently while offering you an opportunity to scan the room to see who may need a bit more support with rhyming.

It's important to practice rhyming a lot until every student can hear and produce rhyming words easily. The ability to recognize rhyming words, even if children are making nonsense words, is a reliable predictor of success for early reading. This makes sense. If a child can't tell that "sat" rhymes with "rat," it would be difficult to distinguish between many words with other closely related sounds (red/rid, pen/pan, leave/live). For that same reason, it's important to always allow children to offer nonsense words when asked for a rhyme (snap/drap, fit/rit, hop/gop). The correct rhyming pattern, even with a nonword, shows the student understands what a rhyme is and can hear it. That allowance makes this much easier for students with less vocabulary and especially for students who may just be hearing and learning English for the first time.

Rhyming games are as ubiquitous as they are fun. We've listed some sources at the end of the chapter, but many of you will know your own. Children find rhyming fun once they get the hang of it.

One of the valuable side effects of practicing lots of rhyming games is providing a clear signal to you regarding those students who will need to be supported more in the phonological awareness activities and with foundational skills in general. There is clear research showing children who struggle with rhymes often have problems with early reading. If you have children who still cannot identify or produce rhymes after everyone else is a rhyming rock star, you should provide additional tailored (small-group) support and see if you can get early detection screening for any children in that category. Problems caught early get solved earlier, and this is a signal that something is wrong, which will make it more challenging for affected children to learn to read.

Alert, active, and analytical listening is essential to laying the ground for reading success. It's not all children need, of course, but it assists with every other component of learning to read, including phonological awareness. It comes in handy in lots of other parts of life too! Listening discrimination by using environmental sounds, followed by rhyming, is a great way to begin because many students who start out less nimble at these activities will become skilled through lots of fun practice. Students who continue to struggle with these basics alert us early to provide the support they need to thrive as readers.

A note before we go on. Strictly speaking, we're teaching more than phonological awareness in this chapter. We're exploring what words are and what sentences are as well. These concepts are both essential knowledge for children as they learn how to read. They help students understand the power and purpose of what they're doing—an understanding we believe is essential to students and we believe we should provide in our classrooms to every child. But they do go beyond phonological *awareness* and into *processing* sounds in words and *understanding* how words come together in sentences to express something coherent and complete.

Sentence and Word Sorting Games

7. *What Is a Sentence and What It Is Not*: Begin by explaining that a sentence is a group of words that tells you something and also tells you about a connected "who" or a "what"; it holds a complete thought. Here again, you can use some of the books from your read-aloud to read examples of sentences and then ask what the sentence tells you and who or what it is about. Follow this with the same book and create examples of non-sentences, asking students to guess what is missing, for example (from *Bats*), read, "Actually bats are" Ask first if it is a sentence and then why not? What's missing? Then read the full sentence, "Actually, bats are shy and gentle animals." You can expand this through the use of nonsense sentences. They tell you something and who or what it is about ("The helicopter ate my cheese sandwich"). This is a challenge in that students have to distinguish between something that makes no sense but *is* a complete thought. There's a group of words that tells you something (ate my ham sandwich) and who or what (the helicopter) but is still a valid sentence. By doing this, you're asking students to distinguish between form and meaning. This is an essential part of understanding language. The good news is children love this and in every case want to make up their own. So it really is a strong way to develop a sense of what a sentence is and to make something that could be really abstract fun and concrete.

8. *Sentence Relay*: This is better done in small groups but can be introduced whole class. Children will want to have their turns! Have some sentence stems (starters) ready to offer for children who may need more support to get started. You may want to start off with everyone using the same sentence stem: "*When I first wake up, I* ______." Ask everyone to think of one sentence to say to the class. In the first few instances, pick a volunteer for this. After the volunteer says her sentence to the class, call on someone else to name the "who"

or "what" of the sentence and then someone else to say the "what happened." This might take some practice before students get the hang of it. Remember, you can return to any of these games during the year, and students will get more and more skilled. Once you feel students have a good sense of this first stage, introduce the "relay" element. The first student says her sentence, and you write it on the board and repeat it. Then ask if someone else can make another sentence using some of the words from the original sentence. Remind them they can do this by changing anything in the "who" or "what" or in the "what happened" to make a different sentence. Then point out they have a new sentence that means something different because the words are different. Keep altering further and further from that original sentence with more student volunteers. Whenever you end, capture the final sentence and read it to the children to have them compare with to the original. Point out again how the word changes made the difference and how changing words or changing the sequence of words changes the meaning of a sentence.

Moving through sound games to this work of distinguishing between words and sentences develops critical language skills and critical thinking! Learning that words that are meaningfully tied together into one idea are a sentence is its own important goal. Learning the inverse—that sentences are made up of purposefully grouped individual words—is valuable. These all serve to move the target toward being able to hear the sounds *inside* words.

Focusing at the Word Level: A Quick Aside

Reading instruction in our country has not always paid enough attention to words either here in foundational skills or in providing children the best ways to grow their vocabularies deeply and broadly. We don't see vocabulary instruction as distinct. We always see it as a "both/and." Although growing children's vocabulary is not part of foundational skills instruction, you'll see our obsession with its importance repeatedly as you read this book. We argue this systemic failure (along with not teaching children foundational skills systematically, of course!) is a major source of the persistently weak reading results in the United States. Many children come to school not yet equipped with all this knowledge; without it, they'll almost certainly struggle to become competent readers. We have to provide everyone with the opportunities to develop both the knowledge *and* skills they need to succeed. One of the ways our obsession plays out is we *always* will ask you to keep vocabulary growth in mind and teach children the meaning of words used even in a game if you suspect it may be new to many of them.

Chuck Perfetti, a prominent cognitive scientist, has shown in elegant and extensive research that proficient readers know a great deal about words. They know the meaning or multiple meanings of lots of words, how to spell them correctly, how they're pronounced, what part of speech they are, and even something about where the parts of the word came from (morphology). Building this knowledge for all children should start right away in kindergarten or pre-K. Activities similar to what we have described here will get your students well on the way to an active appreciation and understanding of words.

In the space below, write a few sentences about why you think it important and helpful to spend time on what a word is and what a sentence is at such an early age.

Here's our reason why:

Just as adults do, children like to and deserve to know the "why"s of what they're learning. Why is reading so valuable? Why are the parts of it important? Words are the names we give to every idea and thing we know. Sentences are the units of meaning when we speak or write to one another. Children should have this awareness because it is part of what literate people have absorbed. They should have it so they are even more motivated to join the ranks of people who read and write and use words and sentences with full confidence. Merriam-Webster defines skill as, "the ability to use one's knowledge effectively and readily in execution or performance." Learning to read is a skill, but underneath the ability to exercise that skill is a great deal of knowledge of phonemes, words, and sentences but also of language in general. Last, we should make sure we cultivate all this in our classrooms because not all children are in a position to receive this awareness in their own homes.

Syllable Games

This next set of games will move students from sentences and words as wholes to being aware of the parts of words: syllables, the first sounds in a word (the onset), and the rest of the word (the rime). Last, they will come to hear and identify discrete phonemes, the discrete sounds inside a word.

The stakes are high on getting students comfortable with syllables soon after they start school. Many of the struggles of weak readers in older grades are often exclusively with multisyllabic words. Preparing students early on with oral activities with syllables will help prevent this. Syllables are the important first steps into breaking down for children what is inside of a word.

9. *Counting Syllables*: The place to start is with students' names. Start with a student whose name has two syllables, say, Henry. Say it very *slowly* at first emphasizing the two syllables but with the correct syllable accented, in this case the first (HEN/ry) to make sure children recognize their names! Ask students how many parts or sections they hear. The first few times you play, do this until you've gotten to every student, then begin again by having students come up to the front to lead the class in separating the syllables of their own names. Be sure to do first and last names. You can expand on this by having students clap each syllable or, more actively, do the same with jumping the syllables. As with many of these activities, this can be beautifully integrated into transitions in and out of the room, to and from the rug. "All students whose first name has two syllables, go get your coats and stand by the door. If you have one syllable in your last name . . ." You may have to help students with multisyllabic names, which is fun for all students.

10. *Find the Syllables*: This is an equally easy, equally fun game. You give a number and ask students to find and point to some object in the room that has that number of syllables in its name. You can make it more exciting if you give a time limit. Some students will figure out they can "find" a classmate! Or even you.

11. *Segmenting and Blending*: The simplest version of this, and likely the most powerful, is to give every student two manipulatives (Legos, blocks, Unifix cubes, anything you have handy) to hold in their hands. Pick a two-syllable word and say it clearly and slowly, emphasizing the syllables while you hold a manipulative in each hand to model the two distinct sounds being separated. Then say the word without the sharp segmentation and push the objects in your hands back together. Have the students try this, first with the same word and then with many

other two-syllable words. Once you graduate to words of three or more syllables, students should be seated at tables or desks so they can have the right number of manipulatives for the number of syllables you're working with. Legos or Unifix cubes are ideal for this activity because the feel of the snapping together emphasizes the syllables coming together to make a word. Breaking the blocks apart emphasizes that the word is built from these sections called syllables.

There are numerous other activities to make students aware of syllables: reassembling pictures cut out from magazines and into as many pieces as that object has syllables, marching in time with syllables, putting students in pairs with instructions to take turns saying a word by clearly breaking it into its syllables and asking their partners how many syllables they heard and then switching. The possibilities, as with much of phonological awareness, are endless.

At this point, all your students should understand and be able to express some version of these ideas:

- A sentence is a group of words that is one complete idea and has someone or something doing some action.
- The meaning of the sentence changes if the words change or the order of the words changes.
- Every word is made of one or more syllables.

Onsets and Rimes

Take those syllables and break them apart further. That's the next step toward phonemic awareness. Your children don't need to know this technical stuff; they just need to play the games and develop their aural discrimination. But you need to know the basics so you model well for your students. An onset and a rime are what we get when we break a syllable apart. The onset is everything that appears before the first vowel, so in *fast* the onset is /f/, in *chill* the onset is /ch/, and in *spring* the onset is /spr/. If there is no consonant before the first vowel in the syllable, then that syllable is not considered to have an onset. For example, *in* and *at* start with vowels; there is nothing before the vowel, so these words don't have an onset. They only have a rime.

The rime is everything in the syllable after the onset, so in *fast* the rime is -ast, in *chill* the rime is -ill, and in *spring* the rime is -ing. You've probably now figured out the relationship between rime and rhyme! You may have also figured out words with the same rime are word families when reading (*sight, light, and fight; rain, pain, and gain; slap, cap, and tap*). Did you notice that if every syllable has a rime that also means every syllable must contain a vowel?

Here's a chart to make it clearer:

Example Word	**Onset**	**Rime**
Fast	F-	-ast
Chill	Ch-	-ill
Spring	Spr-	-ing
It (in)	—	-it (in)

Teaching students to identify onsets and rimes with oral games is similar to having them isolate individual phonemes, so we'll combine the games in the phoneme section. To connect this to later stages of foundational reading: Both these skills are tucked up closely against students beginning to read, first with small words (consonant, vowel, consonant [CVC] words).

This chapter is making a journey through the elements of phonological awareness from largest to smallest. Onset and rime are next to the smallest elements in spoken language. What comes next is the smallest. And the most important of all for successful decoding.

Phonemes and Phonemic Awareness

Enter the phoneme.

Phonemes are the basis of good foundational skills reading instruction. They are the basis for two reasons. First, they are the smallest unit of spoken language that we can perceive, so if we are to fully understand language we need to understand what a phoneme is (and learn to hear it!) because we need to understand all the other parts of spoken language. More importantly, phonemes help us understand the relationship among words, letters, and sounds.

Let's take a quick look.

The word *mat* has three letters each representing a different phoneme (the smallest unit of spoken language we can perceive), and each letter represents one phoneme: 'm' represents the /m/[6] sound (the /m/ phoneme), 'a' represents the /a/ phoneme, and 't' represents the /t/ phoneme. For this word, there is a one-to-one correspondence between each letter and the phoneme it represents. This is why so many programs begin with CVC words. They are straightforward. Many words don't have a one-to-one correspondence

[6] Reminder! Throughout the book, when we refer to a sound, that sound will be inside slashes: /m/ is the sound the letter 'm' makes. When we refer to a letter *name*, the letter will be in quotes: 'm.' When we use a word example, the word will be in *italics: mat.*

between phonemes and letters (also called graphemes). The word *paid* has four letters but three phonemes: /p/, /ā/ (long 'a'), and /d/. In this case, two letters represent one phoneme.

Now your turn. How many phonemes are in the word *weigh*? Again, *paid* has three phonemes: /p/, /ā/, and /d/ but four letters because 'a' and 'i' combine to make the /ā/ sound. In this case, two letters represent one phoneme. Were you right with *weigh*? It's another weird example. *Weigh* has only two phonemes: /w/ made by the 'w' and /ā/ made by the four letters 'eigh.' There are (of course) many and more complex examples of this. If the correspondences were all straightforward, learning to read would be easy. They're not, so it's not. Your students don't need to learn these spelling patterns yet. Remember, they are playing with sound discrimination and learning to identify what sounds they're hearing.

To help in our quest to help children both understand the English language and be able to read and use it, it's useful to remember that spoken words are made from the phonemes that blend together to create a meaningful unit. To decode these words in print, students must unlock the code by matching phonemes with the letters. But before this can happen, children must be aware of the phonemes in their language. This is where you come in!

Before going on to the next section, do the activity below. It would be great if you could find a buddy to make this activity auditory. You could ask your buddy to read the samples to you while you try to work it out through

Onset and Rime: Identify the onset and then the rime. Then swap out the onset phoneme to make a new word.

Hat ______________________________

Sock ______________________________

Shirt ______________________________

Gnash ______________________________

Sentences: How many words? How many syllables? Number of onsets? Rimes? (Bonus: # of phonemes?)

The sun is shining. ______________________

The octopus has eight tentacles and lives in the ocean.

____

Answers on next page:

> Hat: h- -at; new word: *flat*
> Sock: s- -ock; new word: *clock*
> Shirt: sh- -irt; new word: *dirt*
> Gnash: -gn (should sound like /n/) -ash; new word: *cash*
>
> Sentences: How many words? How many syllables? Number of onsets? Rimes? Bonus: # of phonemes?
>
> The sun is shining. 4 words 5 syllables 4 onsets (not *is*) 5 rimes Bonus: 12 phonemes
>
> The octopus has eight tentacles and lives in the ocean. 10 words 15 syllables 10 onsets (all those vowels in the first syllables!) 15 rimes 36 phonemes (2 in *the*, 7 in *octopus*, 3 in *has*, 2 in *eight*, 7 in *tentacles*, 3 in *and*, 4 in *lives*, 2 in *in*, 2 in *the*, 4 in *ocean*).

Not easy, is it? Let us know if we were right!

Let's Learn How to Teach Children about Phonemes

Teaching children to identify phonemes means helping them attune to the separate phonemes that make up a word and figure out how many distinct sounds there are. Learning to manipulate phonemes includes lots of progressively challenging things: seeing how to combine phonemes to make a word, learning to segment words into their separate phonemes, playing with deleting phonemes from a word and hearing what's left afterward, adding phonemes to a word, and swapping phonemes in a word.

If you do an internet search for "phonemic awareness games," you'll get thousands upon thousands of results at your fingertips. There are plenty of these activities out there, so what we'll do here is give you a sampling of our own "tried and true" games. We'll return to those sample games in the phonics chapter to illustrate the power of phonemic awareness in teaching beginning reading. There, we'll marry phonemes to their matching letter or letter combinations. That's early reading.

How Many Sounds Do You Hear?

This is the basis of a number of activities that can be done with phonemes.

- Pick a word students know with two phonemes, for example, my or to or me.
- Say it very slowly, emphasizing the splitting or segmentation of the two phonemes but without elongating each sound (m—y, t—o, m—ee).
- Ask students how many sounds they hear in this word.
- Repeat this a few more times with other two-phoneme words (tea, tie, and, two, up, high, etc.). There is a resource at the end of the chapter with a list of common words organized by the number of phonemes they contain.
- After you've modeled this for a while and students are starting to have a feel for hearing the two sounds, give out manipulatives and ask them to put in front of them the number of objects that match the number of sounds they hear.
- Again, when you see most students able to match objects to sounds, make it harder by moving to the same activity with words with three phonemes and then four.
- If you have different-colored manipulatives (blocks, Legos, Unifix cubes), have students use a different color for each phoneme.
- Be sure to mix things up so that students are engaging in segmenting phonemes each time (instead of only three-phoneme words at a time).

Note: Consonant blends, two consonants together that have two distinct sounds (/cl/, /br/, /st/, etc.) are harder for all of us to recognize as two phonemes. So it is better to leave this until you feel students are proficient with more straightforward patterns.

Pushing Sounds Together (Blending): Part One (with Two Phonemes)

Keep in mind the same list of words with only two phonemes.

- Explain to the children you're going to be pushing sounds together to make words and showing that with objects. Teachers often call this blending.
- Give everyone two of the manipulatives. They will again each represent different phonemes.
- Pick a word (*sigh*) and carefully say each sound separately (s—/igh [/ī/]) while you hold your two manipulatives away from each other.
- Then say the two sounds more quickly (s-igh [/ī/]) while you push your own manipulatives toward each other. (Make sure you move from the *children's* left to right and not your own. You're reinforcing the left to right directionality of reading here!)

- Once you've brought the manipulatives completely together, pronounce the word naturally.
- Repeat your demonstration three or four times with it while you observe how well the students are doing the same actions.
- Then branch out to other words, and have the students repeat the phonemes while they use their objects to demonstrate the sounds pushing together to form a word. Stick with two-phoneme words until your students show mastery—a good long time.
- Once you get to three- and four-phoneme words, you and the children will have to have flat surfaces to work on.

Cutting Out a Sound in a Word

As you may have already guessed, this is saying a word slowly and emphasizing each sound and then taking one sound away. You then ask your students to figure out what sounds are left over.

- Start with words with two or three phonemes, for example, see, hi, or sit.
- Say "sit": take away the /s/ sound.
- Ask students what is left.
- They should be able to figure out it's "it."
- Keep it simple at first, with two- and three-phoneme words. And wait a while before you have children wrestle with words like "stop."

Once students are good at cutting out initial phonemes, you can start to play the game with cutting final phonemes.

Pushing or Blending Sounds Together: Part Two (with Onsets and Rimes)

You're going to do the same thing you did with phonemes but with onsets and rimes.

- Start with CVC words and with a common word family such as –at.
- Offer a variety of different onsets while you stick with the same rime (word family) at first.
- As students get better, hop around rapidly to different word families and get trickier with longer or less common words, being sure to always provide the meaning for words students might not know!
- Make these into riddles and have students guess:

  "If I take the /k/ sound of 'coats,' I have something horses eat. What is it?" (oats).

  "Now if I take 'oats' and put a /b/ sound in front of it, I have things that float. What are they?" (boats, and bonus points to any child who notices 'floats' also rhymes).

Mixing It All Up

Once students are comfortable doing one of these activities in isolation, you can start to mix the games up.

- Pull sounds apart, then push them together in rapid succession with different groups and amounts of phonemes.
- Play with pulling onsets off harder and harder rimes.
- Then play with pulling rimes off onsets and swapping in a different rime:
  "Take the –at off 'bat.' What do you have left?" (b).
  "Put an 'oy' after the 'b.' What new word do you have?" (boy).

The possibilities and variations are endless. And remember internet searches if you aren't using the Adams book or another resource! There are lots of creative teachers who have developed lots of fun games for all phases of phonological awareness.

A Caution for This Work and Another Word on "Upcoming Attractions"

The order in which children learn to recognize and identify phonemes aurally (which is initial sounds first, then final sounds, and last medial [middle] sounds), is the same order they will learn to spell when they get to phonics instruction. So it is *really* important to stick with that order when you play these games. It is developmentally aligned with how children's understanding and abilities grow and is consistent with the scientific community's findings on how reading proficiency is acquired. So have fun, but follow the science!

A Word on Assessing Phonological and Phonemic Awareness

Observing your students carefully during all the activities described in this chapter can give you immediate insight into whether or not your children are mastering these skills. This is easier when you're working in small groups, but if you're disciplined about tracking and recording who is and who isn't mastering a given skill, assessing in the moment can work whole class as well. This is especially true because all of these activities should be done repeatedly over a period of months. How many times you do an activity before you retire it depends upon your class's ability to pick up the skill and the challenge of a given activity. Once you've done any activity for a number of days, you will get a sense of which children need more support and practice. These should definitely happen in small-group work so you can give children who need it more opportunities to practice and more feedback.

There are also many more formal assessments available, some free or inexpensive. Our favorite is the one at the back of *Phonemic Awareness in Young Children* (Adams, 1998). It is comprehensive and easy to administer.

Points to consider when doing phonological awareness activities:

- One of the hardest but most critical skills you have to develop is the ability to pronounce phonemes precisely. If you don't, you'll confuse your students. This takes practice. There's a natural tendency to drag out many consonants ('b,' 'c/k,' 'd,' 'g,' 'h,' 'p,' 'm,' and 't' to name just a few) with an 'uh' sound—also known as the "schwa" sound. So /b/ becomes /buh/ if you don't pay close attention. The schwa sound is a real sound in words made by different vowels (think of the /a/ in *sofa* or the /o/ in *occur*. But it is NOT a sound in the word *bat*, so you don't want to give students the impression it is by sloppy pronunciation! The best trick we know to get in the habit is to consciously exhale before you say a consonant sound and then say the consonant right at the end of your breath. You'll have no breath left to add the 'uh' so your /b/ will come out crisp and clear. If you don't learn this essential skill, the results are likely going to be /buh/, /ah/, and /duh/ for your students! There are links to a couple of very good videos in the resources section at the end of the chapter.

- Children need to learn how to articulate English, too. They need to know how to pronounce the phonemes precisely and accurately as well. This is true for all children but essential if children can speak another language, which has its own phonemes, some different from English pronunciation. So when you're working with phonemic awareness, help students pay attention to what their mouths and tongues need to do to shape the sound accurately. Help them see what their face looks like, what the sound feels like in the throat or mouth or on the tongue. Having a few mirrors around the room can be helpful. However you do it, provide practice time for accurate pronunciation for children as well as you!

- The inverse: It is hard to hear phonemes! *Especially* vowel sounds and the sounds in the middle of syllables. This becomes even harder for adults, who are often mentally picturing the spelling of words (so visualizing letters) rather than isolating the sounds. Be patient with your students and with yourself when it comes to hearing phonemes. Don't be alarmed. Practice more. Reading is magical, but it's not natural. *That is true even if you yourself have forgotten how you learned to read so it seems natural to you!* Hearing and recognizing the sounds inside words is hard work. Matching those sounds to the letters, the subject of later chapters, is even harder. This foundation of phonemic awareness you're setting sets the stage for success with phonics.

- Remember, these activities are just samples to give you a sense of phonological awareness and the nature of the activities you can do with students. We chose activities that needed few if any materials. Many activities ask for game boards or are games students can play quasi-independently in centers or small groups and tend to be more elaborate than the ones we've offered.
- Phonological awareness activities present lots of opportunities to develop expressive language as students volunteer answers. It's important to hold students accountable to speak in full sentences so they get in the habit, as is appropriate for the activities you're engaging in.
- Equally important is seizing the opportunity to teach your students the meaning of words you use in playing phonemic awareness games that may be new to them. It only takes a few seconds to define these simple, mostly concrete words, and your students will benefit greatly.
- Nearly all of these activities can be used during transition times or when moving from place to place. That will reinforce learning and will create smoother transitions as well. Phonological awareness games are your classroom management friends! In our school, whenever the kindergarteners went through the halls, their teachers would walk backward facing them and model blending two phonemes by bringing her hands together. The students would do the same. Many of the other activities (clapping syllables, adding and deleting onsets) will work just as well. To combine smooth transitions with assessing, have each student do an activity solo before going to line up or get dressed for recess or head to snack. Here's an example: Have all students stand and face a partner. The partner whose
- first name comes first in alphabetical order says a two-syllable word; the other partner says another one. When both are finished, line up.
- Phonological awareness is ideal for pre-K as well as kindergarten, although some activities will need more repetition and take more time to get started. Younger students will respond as well as kindergarten students, and any pre-K classes we've worked with have loved the positive energy and activity of these games.
- Phonemic awareness work can and should be done in pre-K and kindergarten but revisited for the first month or so in first grade or later if children need it. Revisit it in later grades for any children who

need the extra support. This can be done along with phonics work because these activities reinforce each other. Mastery of phonemic awareness is essential to reading success!

- Remember the value of using nonsense words along with real words when you play phonemic awareness games (this will continue into phonics work, too). Part of the reason for mixing nonsense words with real English words is it gives children equal access to the sounds of English without worrying about anything else. Another benefit is it expands how many different sound combinations children can be exposed to. And finally, students with smaller vocabularies will not lose out on the benefits of this work.
- We've found many core English Language Arts programs do not do enough phonological awareness work. Given its importance, and the research connecting it to successful early reading, this is not okay. If that's your situation, we recommend you use what we provided as a starting off point. Then find more activities so you can give your students at least 15–20 minutes a day of phonological awareness work until they demonstrate mastery.

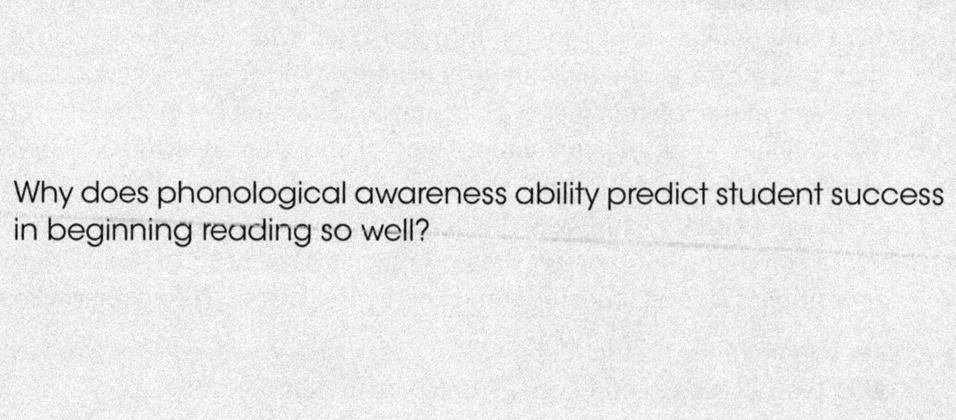

Why is phonological awareness work so helpful to beginning readers?

Why does phonological awareness ability predict student success in beginning reading so well?

Sources for Deeper Learning and Teaching

Chart of two-, three-, and four-phoneme words

http://blog.maketaketeach.com/wp-content/uploads/2016/01/Phoneme-Segmentation-Cheat-Sheet.pdf

Chart of four- to six-phoneme words

https://www.readingresource.net/support-files/phonemes.pdf

Videos to help you pronounce phonemes precisely and accurately

This video, from Rollins University's Center for Language and Literacy, is excellent and efficient. Many of the examples are British speakers of English, but the person modeling in this video uses US articulation and models beautifully. There are close-up shots of her mouth so you can see what happens to the lips, tongue, and mouth when pronouncing different phonemes.

https://www.google.com/search?rlz=1C1GGRV_enUS751US751&q=youtube+44+phonemes&sa=X&ved=2ahUKEwjVn_T-kOjfAhXtYN8KHRhxCyYQ1QIoAXoECAYQAg&biw=1517&bih=695

Learning to pronounce phonemes precisely is really important for your students and takes lots of practice and study.

https://www.youtube.com/watch?v=IwJx1NSineE

Children who speak another language have many advantages, but they also have to deal with two sets of phonemes at times.

Reading Rockets has lots of good information about reading in general, and we found this article a very good discussion of the importance of this work for children who need to learn the English phonemes.

http://www.readingrockets.org/article/what-does-research-tell-us-about-teaching-reading-english-language-learners

Activities for Phonemic Awareness Growth

Stand Up/Sit Down: Turn word sorts into an opportunity for movement. "Stand up if you hear a word with—" or "sit down if you see the sound—" can add movement to a basic task.

High-Five Your Neighbor: Same as above, with the task to high-five a neighbor if they hear (phonemic awareness) or see (phonics) the given sound.

If You're Happy and You Know It: Turn a task into a song by setting it to the lyrics of kid-friendly tunes, e.g., "If you hear /s/ and you know it, clap your hands" or "If you think you know the word, yell it out!"

Do You Speak Robot? Turn your blending routine into a game by teaching students that you (or a puppet!) speak robot: one sound at a time. Students must listen to the segmented sounds and blend them together to understand the words.

Do You Speak Snail? Turn your blending routine into another game by teaching students to "speak snail." Say words slowly, sound by sound. Students have to "guess" the word or "translate snail speak" by blending them together.

Let's Hear It For: Teach students to spell high-frequency words, or to learn word parts, by cheering for each letter, cheerleader style. "Give me an A!" "I've got your A! I've got your A!"

Head, Shoulders, and Toes: Blend or segment words with a physical activity: students touch their heads for the first sound, their shoulders for the middle sound, and their toes for the end sound of three-phoneme words. (Note: This task can be adapted for syllables or more parts can be added for more sounds.)

Whisper It, Shout It: Vary any oral activity by simply varying the volume level for students when they are responding. Alternating between whispering and shouting or adding other silly additions (say it like you're under water, say it in slow motion, mouth it with no sound) can bring the fun to a simple task.

Snap/Clap/Stomp When You Hear: Give students a physical activity to do when they hear a sound and spelling pattern, rhyming word, or other stated task.

Freeze Dance: Play music and let students dance. Have them freeze when they hear a given sound and spelling pattern, rhyming word, or other stated task.

Note: These enhancements should be added to lessons that reflect current skills. Students do not need to repeatedly practice what they have already mastered. So, either retire an old favorite or repurpose it to reflect new learning.

Works Consulted

Adams, M. (1990). *Beginning to read: Thinking and learning about print.* Cambridge, MA: MIT Press.

Adams, M. (1998). *Phonemic awareness in young children.* Baltimore, MD: Brookes Publishing.

Bus, A. G., & van IJzendoorn, M. H. (1999). Phonological awareness and early reading: A meta-analysis of experimental training studies. *Journal of Educational Psychology, 91*(3), 403–414.

Cunningham, A. E., & Stanovich, K. E. (1998). What reading does for the mind. *American Educator, 22*, 8–15.

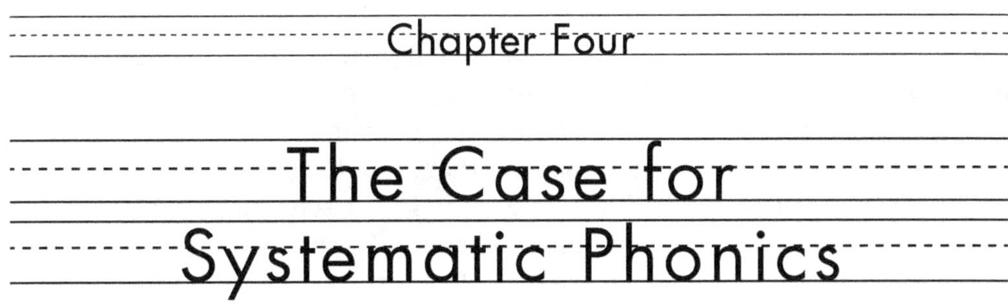

Chapter Four

The Case for Systematic Phonics

The Origins of the Alphabetic Principle: A Story

This story is David's.

I tried to encourage (within reason and with each teacher's blessing) children to come to my office with any questions or accomplishments they had. I always promised that if I were otherwise engaged or couldn't answer them at the time I'd get back to them and said when. This didn't result in long lines at the office but rather a set of regular customers, tending toward the "antsy" end of the spectrum. One day in mid-October, Marvin appeared at my door with a classmate, Angel, in tow. Marvin was a big, likable first-grader who lived with his equally lovable paternal grandparents. School did not come easily to Marvin. It soon became clear he had drafted Angel, the lively, outspoken *de facto* class leader, to accompany him as his advocate. Marvin was an earnest, hardworking child who was struggling mightily with reading and needed lots of repetition to master each of the phonics patterns introduced to date. He'd gotten that repetition through games, puzzles, and worksheets and was making good progress.

His reading group had just finished learning short vowels, and his teacher was starting to introduce long vowels. Although Marvin and his group had struggled with short vowels, they did all master them and had all recently passed our short-vowel assessment. After some brief celebrations, they were ready and needed to move on.

Turned out Marvin was not, hence the visit to my office. After all his work to master short vowels, he refused to believe that 'a' would now sometimes make a different sound in words and had asked to come talk to Mr. Liben because he didn't believe this was, in fact, true and was seeking a second adult opinion. As smart and deep a thinker as Marvin was, he often struggled to find the right words for what he wanted to say. His vocabulary hadn't yet caught up with his powerful mind. We know weak oral language stores in young children make learning to read harder simply because they have fewer words to draw on and less experience listening and saying a large variety of words with a large variety of sounds in them. Oral language, however, is not the same as intelligence; Marvin was plenty smart and pragmatic. Thus, he had enlisted Angel, the smoothest-talking first-grader of them all, to help present his case. When the boys stated their grievance, I realized this would take time and told Marvin and his lawyer that I would come by and talk to the whole class about this valuable question. Before I sent them back to class, I showed them a world map, pointed to where Syria and Lebanon are, and said thousands of years ago those countries weren't there and there was another big country named Phoenicia in that part of the world. I told the boys to remember that because it had a lot to do with the answer. As they left the room, I heard Angel say, "Mr. Liben is weird."

I prepared a much-abridged history of the alphabet for our first-graders and negotiated with the first-grade teachers for part of their read-aloud time for a couple of days. I wanted them to have a sense of why reading was so complicated *and* so worthwhile. We'll return to Martin and Angel and their classmates shortly.

What Is Phonics and Why Has It Been So Controversial?

If you do a dictionary hunt, you will more likely find something like "a method of teaching people to read and pronounce words by learning the sounds of letters, letter groups, and syllables" (Merriam-Webster). Other definitions might not include syllables, and some would object to "sounds of letters" as opposed to something like the "sounds letters or combinations of letters represent." That being said, the general idea is pretty straightforward. Yet educators often have very different and strongly held beliefs about almost anything that touches on phonics. If you've been in education for a while, or read much about it, you know there has always been controversy. There are heated debates in the literacy world and markedly more in early literacy (how many furious battles about how to teach twelfth-grade English have you heard?). The disagreements over the rightful role, intensity of focus, and approach within the phonics universe is a central part of these "Reading Wars."

Phonics brings together in one place educators' ideas and more importantly our *beliefs* about literacy, literature, young children, how structured teaching of young children should be, how much children should practice newly acquired skills, how and what to assess, and who's accountable for children learning to read. A perfect storm in short. The controversy is not new! Beliefs going back at least to Horace Mann, the "father of the Common [universal public] School, who in the 1840s referred to the letters of the alphabet as 'skeleton-shaped, bloodless ghostly apparitions'" (lecture before the American Institute, 1841).

Have no fear; we'll resolve it in the next few pages!

If you teach early readers with systematic phonics, you'll support children in understanding how specific letters or letter combinations represent sounds in order to read. If not, you're likely using some form of whole-word learning, as the name implies, focusing on the entire word and relying on the context or syntax of sentences. It was letters, and by implication the sounds they represent, that repulsed Horace Mann, not words. So for much of education after the mid-19th century when (because as with much in education, there have always been cycles of "innovation") schools did not teach children phonics; they taught some version of Whole Word instruction, *Dick and Jane* books being the most well-known examples. *Dick and Jane* used text controlled by simple words, supportive context, pictures, and lots of repetition.

You can get a sense from this sample in Figure 1.

"Look, Jane," said Dick.
"Here is something funny.
Can you guess what it is?"

"Oh, yes," said Jane.
"I can guess.
I can guess what it is.
This will help me find Sally."

FIGURE 1. From *We Come and Go* (1968). (Penguin Random House. Used by permission.)

So Whole Word teaching moved instruction outward away from letter–sound relationships to the word rather than any of its parts. In the 1970s, Frank Smith, a Canadian cognitive psychologist, and Kenneth and Yetta Goodman, teacher educators at Arizona State, did for Whole Word instruction what Whole Word instruction did for phonics—it swept it away from mainstream early grade reading instruction. They broadened their attention away from the whole word to the whole *language* and advocated that reading should be more like a "guessing game" where children used context and picture clues to guess what the words were. Over a number of years, this started a movement called—you guessed it—Whole Language.

In Whole Language approaches, the theory is the child learns to read from the entire word in the context of whatever story or trade book they pick up. Whole Language moved away from letters and sounds *and* words to embrace language holistically, arguing that learning to read and write was as natural as learning to talk. This led to changes in the texts used for instruction in foundational skills and changes in methods as well.

Texts used in phonics instruction, sometimes called decodables, used a combination of words containing phonics patterns already taught or currently being taught and high-frequency words taught as wholes. These high-frequency words, sometimes referred to as "sight words" may be phonetically irregular (his, where, their, the, etc.) and show up so frequently in text that they need to be explicitly taught and practiced until mastered. This led, especially in kindergarten and early first grade (where children hadn't been exposed to many phonics patterns yet), to texts with lots of pigs doing jigs and dogs that jog and cats who sat on mats. Whole Word "Primers," as evidenced by *Dick and Jane*, were not that much more stimulating. Both types of text were controlled. Whole Language texts, in contrast, attempted to dispense with any type of control and instead use authentic books, ideally trade literature. The reason for this was, as the name implied, access to natural language as a whole is the best way to teach children to read. Because children learn language "naturally" and reading is as natural as talking, reading can also be learned "naturally" and foundational skills like the sound–letter patterns of English can be absorbed just by lots of independent reading.

The quotes below are quotes from well-known Whole Language theorists:[1]

- *All proficient readers have acquired an implicit knowledge of how to read, but this knowledge has been developed through the practice of reading, not through anything that is taught at school.*
- *The child is already programmed to learn to read.*
- *Children can develop and use an intuitive knowledge of letter–sound correspondences [without] any phonics instruction [or] without any deliberate instruction from adults.*
- *Literacy learning proceeds naturally . . .*
- *(It is) . . . through using language and hearing others use it in everyday situations that children learn to talk. Our research has indicated that the same is true of learning to read and write.*
- *No one will teach your child how to read. Reading isn't taught. Reading is developed. . . . They have learned how to speak—a much more difficult process—and they will learn how to read! All you have to do is set the right conditions.*

Here's a problem with all that. Estimates of when *Homo sapiens* started

[1] In order: 1) Frank Smith (1973). *Psychology and reading.* New York, NY: Holt, Rinehart & Winston. 2) ibid. 3) *(p. 86) Weaver, C. (1980). Psycholinguistics and reading.* Cambridge, MA: Winthrop. 4) National Council of Teachers of English. (1993). *Elementary school practices.* Retrieved from http://ncte.org. 5) Schickendanz, J. A. (1986). *More than the ABC's: The early stages of reading and writing.* Washington, DC: NAEYC. 6) Failure Free Reading (2005). 30 Ways to Improve Your Child's Reading. See http://www.failurefree.com/downloads/30Ways.pdf.

talking to one another range from 50,000 to over a million years ago. We've been using symbols written on a surface to stand for the sounds we hear within those words to try to communicate with one another for less than 5,000 years. Children who can hear and make controlled noises *do* universally learn to talk and understand speech. Judging from our persistently terrible results anytime we evaluate American schoolchildren, National Assessment of Educational Progress (NAEP) results consistently show us we have a majority of our children who are *not* reading and writing with any degree of proficiency.

We experienced this full blast for ourselves at the Family Academy in our first couple of years. We opened our doors in the fall of 1991, during the zenith of the Whole Language movement, right down the hill from Teachers College Columbia University, the East Coast epicenter of the movement. None of us remembered how we learned to read. The natural ethos of Whole Language sounded right to us. We're zealous people, hardworking and sincere. So we did *everything* right for Whole Language instruction. You'll remember from the introduction how that worked out for us and our first cohort of children.

We set up a print-rich environment (labeling every object with its name ("sink," "cabinet," "blocks," "water table," etc.), we read aloud great books, we talked about books, we celebrated books, and we devoted lots of time to free-choice reading and journaling and, in general, developed a culture of literacy. The school was a joyous place for sure, built, we thought, around literacy.

Of course, some teachers had always done these kinds of rich classroom literacy practices, and most parents made sure to do these sorts of things with their own children at home. But the Whole Language movement brought this type of rich environment, as well as a valuing of inventive spelling and student voice (the child "invents" the spelling of a word based on the sounds she hears so she can write freely) into classes throughout the country. These aspects of Whole Language were, without qualification, a needed and welcome change.

The problem was that was about the extent of it. Specifics stopped with the print-rich guidance because everything else would just fall into place. The lack of attention paid to teaching children to read made total sense because the core belief was that reading was as natural as breathing or talking. That meant the texts used for instructing beginning readers and the methods used with those texts were fairly haphazard.

Here's how it went. In a Whole Language approach, if children couldn't recognize or sound out a word, they were encouraged to skip it with the idea that, as with language in general, at some point when the child was ready she would learn it. Similarly, if a child misread a word but it didn't alter the meaning of the sentence much (for example substituting "starving" for "hungry" in "Sam burst into the room yelling, 'I'm so hungry!'"), teachers were told not to intervene.

Over time, some educational publishers did start to make highly predictable texts, complete with Big Books, that were marketed as Whole Language

FIGURE 2. McGraw-Hill Education Wright Group. Used with Permission..

series, especially for kindergarten and early first grade (some of you may remember The Wright Group's *Mrs. Wishy Washy* and company). Because they were highly controlled texts, they provided more support than picture books or other trade books. Ironically, these materials used similar patterns of repeated words and repetitive sentence structure the *Dick and Jane* books had a couple of generations earlier. Figure 2 shows a page from *Mrs. Wishy Washy*.

Whole Language was, of course, completely hostile to the systematic or even casual study of phonics, the ultimate segmenting of the written language. Many instructional materials, district policies, school administrations, and Schools of Education told teachers not to even encourage children to sound out words. In many settings, phonics instruction became the exclusive domain of the special education classrooms, where the children who hadn't learned to read via Whole Language were disproportionately placed.

Education movements have often been driven by large states that control material adoption at the central level. California's embrace of Whole Language and the adoption of nothing but Whole Language programs in 1987 helped accelerate the movement, and by the early 1990s, right when we started the Family Academy, it was pretty much everywhere. However, just as California helped the growth of Whole Language, it was pivotal in bringing it to an end. By the time of the release of the 1991 NAEP results, California's fourth-graders were next to last, ahead of only Guam. Low scores in California and elsewhere, as well as fourth-grade NAEP reading scores declining during the 1980s and 1990s, caused many people to start to question Whole Language as an effective approach. California pivoted back to a systematic phonics approach in 1996.[2] Advocates of phonics had been raising the alarm all along, but these scores heated the debate and led to full-scale engagement in what has been called the "Reading Wars," which lasted through the 1990s.

When things are going relatively well in our country, the federal government

[2] For a quick and fascinating history of California's failed experiment with Whole Language, see this *New York Times* article from 1996: https://www.nytimes.com/1996/05/22/us/california-leads-revival-of-teaching-by-phonics.html.

pays more attention to education. So in 1997, as the Reading Wars raged, Congress commissioned the National Reading Panel (NRP) to "evaluate existing research and evidence to find the best ways of teaching children to read." The panel consisted of 14 experts in reading education, psychology, and higher education, and one parent. The panel members combed through hundreds of studies to choose the 75 that met their strict criteria of high-quality scientifically sound research. They published their report in 2000, and it remains a gold standard for reading research.

These are some of the major conclusions about systematic phonics:

- ". . . systematic phonics instruction makes a bigger contribution to children's growth in reading than alternative programs providing unsystematic or no phonics instruction" (NRP, 2-92).
- "The conclusion supported by these findings is that various types of systematic phonics approaches are significantly more effective than non-phonics approaches in promoting substantial growth in reading" (ibid, 2-93).
- ". . . systematic phonics instruction is effective when delivered through tutoring, through small groups, and through teaching classes of children (ibid).
- "Phonics instruction produces the biggest impact on growth in reading when it begins in kindergarten or 1st grade. . . . These results indicate clearly that systematic phonics instruction in kindergarten and 1st grade is highly beneficial and that children at these developmental levels are quite capable of learning phonemic and phonics concepts. To be effective, systematic phonics instruction introduced in kindergarten must be appropriately designed for learners and must begin with foundational knowledge involving letters and phonemic awareness" (ibid).
- ". . . systematic phonics instruction is significantly more effective than non-phonics instruction in helping to prevent reading difficulties among at-risk children and in helping to remediate reading difficulties in disabled readers" (ibid, 2-94).

Despite the comprehensiveness of the NRP report (14 Blue Ribbon experts, two years of research, hundreds of studies), there was still some opposition to its findings although actually less than one might have expected given the intensity of the Reading Wars. That long history of controversy about reading instruction had so many beliefs and emotions swirling around how young children should spend their time in school that the NRP report was surprisingly well received. One of the panel members opposed the conclusions and wrote a minority report, linked with other interesting resources at the end of this chapter. She felt the studies in the panel's reviews were much stronger in connecting systematic phonics to word recognition than they were to comprehension, that literacy instruction needed to be much more than just phonics, and that phonics instruction was all stifling to little children (all "drill and kill").

The NRP report was clear on the question of phonics' weak connection to comprehension in the many studies they reviewed. Just like building a house, there's a lot to reading. Phonics, the central component of foundational reading, forms the bottom layer of the sturdy reading house. It's not the house by itself; it's just the foundation, but the house sure won't stand up without it. Phonics helps a child recognize a word in a text *if* that word is one she knows. If a child doesn't know a word, phonics skill will support the child's *pronouncing* a word correctly (whether out loud or "in her head"), but this would be little help if the child has no idea of what the word means. By the end of first grade, an on-track child with solid phonics skills would probably decode and pronounce "frenzy," "shindig," and "gem" correctly but not know what they mean. Comprehension *is* more than successful decoding; it requires vocabulary, knowledge, motivation, and the confidence to recognize when understanding isn't happening and calling on the right strategies to address the problem.

Here's the rub: Successful decoding doesn't guarantee comprehension, but poor decoding guarantees poor comprehension. In the chapter on fluency, you'll learn that successful decoding doesn't even guarantee fluent reading. But weak decoding guarantees weak fluency, and weak fluency guarantees weak comprehension. A weak foundation makes for a shaky house. So, although critics of the report and opponents of phonics, in general, are right in saying there is much more to comprehension than phonics, they fail to understand that mastering phonics is *necessary* even while not *sufficient*.

We've never really understood the idea that phonics learning needs to be "drill and kill." Even if you have never taught younger grades or taught at all, you might be able to imagine all kinds of games, puzzles, riddles, and even movement ("As soon as you hear a word with the short 'a' sound, jump three times while saying the word, then sit down and spell it to your partner). Besides, learning to read is thrilling to primary grade children. They *all* know that you come to school above all else to learn to read. So doing that biggest-of-all thing is thrilling in itself. Actually understanding how the spoken word translates to words you can actually see, read, and write is heady stuff. The fact that phonics practice is *so* conducive to games, songs, and movement is icing on the cake. But fun and movement spice up everybody's day!

Phonics lessons and practicing the sound–spelling patterns to mastery can be made really fun with just a little effort. The post-college and career readiness standards English Language Arts (ELA) programs we'll be discussing in the appendix all achieve this. To be fair to the minority view member of the NRP though, many phonics programs at the time of the report *were* too drill oriented and did not take advantage of the opportunity for active learning we know phonics learning invites. Materials teachers had to use were dull and uncreative. It's not surprising that many teachers turned their backs on them in favor of the more liberating ideas of Whole Language.

Time to Return to Marvin, Angel, and the Phoenicians

Once their teacher carved out some time for me to come into their class, I started by showing the same map of the Mediterranean and Near East that I had shown Angel and Marvin. I told the class that long ago this is where people started trying to preserve spoken words. This was followed by showing pictures of the earliest hieroglyphics from more than 5,500 ("fifty-five groups of one hundred") years ago (Figure 3).

We then went into small groups to discuss the question of what problems might come up with a system of writing based on pictures. As one child said, "Writing these pictures in clay to say everything you want could take forever!" We then thought together about whether there were some words that were easy to make pictures for and some not so easy. The general consensus was that words such as "dog," "house," and "lady" were pretty easy, but words such as "is," "was," and "who" were not so easy and that making pictures of big numbers could take all day. After a while, everyone agreed that pictures were not a great system of writing.

On my next visit, we talked about Phoenicia. Using a map of the ancient Mediterranean, I pointed out there were a lot of cities in Phoenicia, and they bought and sold things to each other all the time, and when cities or countries do this it is called "trading." We then talked about how in the United States now we also trade, and we compared some of what we trade with what the Phoenician cities traded. I then told them the traders of Phoenicia were having trouble because of the problems with writing that was mostly pictures. I asked the children to pair up and talk about what problems the Phoenicians may have had.

As an aside, we've always found very young children willing to engage with these sorts of sophisticated questions. When asked interesting, challenging

FIGURE 3. Image by José Manuel Benito. No rights reserved.

questions and given a chance to think and talk about it, they'll arrive at answers ranging from silly to profoundly insightful. If the culture of the classroom and, more powerfully, the culture of the whole school encourages this type of reflection and question asking, this sort of curiosity will be nourished and become part of most children's intellectual identity. And how powerful when it is done about the concepts of literacy itself to help children stay in the game when learning is hard work!

Angel (Marvin's "lawyer") was clear on one problem: "If one city didn't get what they paid for, it would be hard to write about it and prove it with pictures." Janet, who loved math *and* reading, added another: "If they wanted to write down that somebody had bought lots of something, like rice, it would be pretty hard to show how much with just pictures." After talking about different examples for a few minutes, it became clear writing was needed to solve problems of all sorts, and pictures sometimes wouldn't work well. Alvin noted, "They must have had a lot of arguments before there was writing." They also started to wonder about books and when books started, which I said firmly had to wait for another time.

The minicourse continued the next day with a picture of the Phoenician alphabet (Figure 4) and an explanation that the Phoenicians were the first to connect a letter to a sound.

I asked the children to look carefully at the Phoenician alphabet and how it compared with their familiar English one. I gave them a hint that something important was missing. They soon realized there were no vowels. I asked, "How did the Phoenicians read and write words without vowels?" and asked them to think about that for a few minutes. It was unlikely anybody would figure this out (and many might quietly be thinking, like Marvin, that it would be GREAT to do away with vowels!). Yet thinking about a problem even without arriving at a solution often helps set the stage for understanding. Their teacher put the following words on the board, read them aloud slowly two times, and asked them to do the same: cake, car, all, sat.

FIGURE 4. Image created by Ansgar for Wikipedia. No rights reserved.

Next, she wrote the words on the board stripped of their 'a's: ck, cr, ll, st. We said sometimes you could use context (the rest of the words) to figure out one word. For example, if the sentence was, "I ate the ck," they could figure "ck" was cake, or if it was "You st down," they knew "st" was sat or sit. We tried this with some longer words and *they soon realized it didn't work so well* (try it!: *th sn rlzd t ddnt wrk s wll)*. I explained that the Phoenicians ended up using some of their consonants to make their vowel sounds. As first-graders learning to read, several of them immediately said, "that would make it really hard to learn to read!"

The children next worked to determine the sound 'a' was making in each of those four words (cake, car, all, sat). The goal was to see the 'a' was sounding different in each word (Marvin and Angel were paying *very* close attention now). We then discussed how the spelling of the word could make 'a' sound different at different times. They all knew "sat," and many children (including Angel) had already studied 'long a' (/ā/) starting with the magic e (consonant-vowel-consonant [cvc]/e) rule so "cake" made sense, which they did their best to explain to Marvin.

I explained that the rule for "car" as in "bar" or even "star" was called a vowel that is "'r' controlled" because the 'r' makes the vowel sound different all the time. Their teacher assured them they would be learning and practicing all these patterns for themselves during the year. We told them letters sometimes have to work extra hard and make different sounds. We reminded them that they knew this from 'C' making both a /k/ and /s/ sound. That was because there are more sounds in the English language than there are letters in our alphabet. And *that* was because English is kind of a "hodgepodge language" that was made up of languages all over the world, just like all our families had come from all over to live in New York and go to Family Academy. So we needed to have combinations of letters to make all of the sounds in all the words we use. This system is really what phonics is and what they were working hard to learn.

I was hoping to end what had evolved into a minicourse with showing how the word "phonics" and "phone" came from Phoenicia because the Phoenicians were the first people known to come up with the idea of connecting letters to sounds. I wanted to show Marvin and Angel that I really wasn't weird!

But of course, the conversation took another turn. One student learning English as a second language asked if this was the same in Spanish, and this led to a discussion of how languages do have different ways to spell sounds; in Spanish it is much easier to learn reading because each letter does always make the same sound because Spanish had fewer other languages mixing in with it than English did. Angel immediately asked if we could show them how that worked. But the philology lessons were done for now. Although we promised that later in the year when they know more English phonics, we can do this with one of our teachers who reads and speaks Spanish way better than Mr. Liben does.

We know that long-ago minicourse would have been impossible without the phonemic awareness work we had instituted in kindergarten. It was also illuminating to realize that in our earliest days as a Whole Language school we *never* had these types of rich discussions about language no matter how much we tried to generate them. That first grade stayed interested in language and would raise many new questions about how language works for years, and it may not be a coincidence that our first child to get her PhD was that same alert Janet who was able to think about the shortcomings of a pictorial system so well.

Nor does phonics have to be bereft of intellectual depth (as our minicourse on the alphabetic principle showed). Learning how to decode—beginning to *read*—is deeply satisfying, deeply intellectual work. It should *never* be mindless. Whenever children decode a word they don't know the meaning of, they should know they can ask about it and learn a new word. When they have trouble pronouncing a word with phonics patterns they haven't yet learned, they should be asked to think of what patterns in the word they do know and say those. Then they should look at the other letters and try to think what letters might be signaling what sounds. This is not easy for young children, and sometimes all of us will provide the not-yet-decodable word, but doing the hard and satisfying work of closely examining how words are put together grows the beginning of an understanding and appreciation of language.

Back to the NRP and the Reading Wars

We came to our own understandings about the role of systematic phonics in a comprehensive reading program at the Family Academy. The question for others, as for us, was how to incorporate the findings of the 2003 NRP report. Regarding foundational reading, as the quotes below make clear, systematic phonics should be a part of but never constitute the entire reading curriculum:

- "Programs that focus too much on the teaching of letter-sounds relations and how to use their constituent sounds to write words, while not enough on putting them to use, are unlikely to be very effective" (NRP, 2-96).
- "In implementing systematic phonics instruction, educators must keep the end in mind and ensure that children understand the purpose of learning letter-sounds and are able to apply their skills in their daily reading and writing activities" (ibid).
- "Finally, it is important to emphasize that *systematic* [emphasis added] phonics instruction should be integrated with other reading instruction to create a balanced reading program. Phonics instruction is never a total reading program" (ibid, 2-97).
- "Phonics should not become the dominant component in a reading program, neither in the amount of time devoted to it nor in the significance attached" (ibid).
- "It is important to evaluate children's reading competence in many

ways, not only by their phonics skills but also by their interest in books and their ability to understand information that is read to them" (ibid).

- "By emphasizing all of the processes that contribute to growth in reading, teachers will have the best chance of making every child a reader" (ibid).

The NRP report remains highly influential and is considered the last word on phonics research as well as many other aspects of reading. It has been cited in academic journals and studies more than 20,000 times since being released. More than 1,000 of those citations came in the year we wrote this book, so its impact isn't fading. It's also worth noting that the United Kingdom, which also went through a Whole Language period with equally devastating outcomes for far too many children, essentially replicated the NRP with British-based studies (they *still* don't trust us here in the colonies!) and got the same results.

You can continue to see extremely strong evidence for the importance of systematic phonics instruction from an important study done nearly 20 years after the NRP report was released.

In 2018, David Paige, an education professor and reading specialist, worked with teachers from 31 of the lowest-performing elementary schools in the lowest-performing district in a populous south-central state. Although some other components of ELA were addressed in the teacher training program of Paige's study, the vast majority of the study's intervention work focused on teachers' *understanding* and implementing systematic phonics. When they were in the spring of third grade, children were given an assessment of basic phonics and fluency. The researchers found that 70% of children who passed the study's assessment of basic phonics and fluency also passed their state reading test. The vast majority (more than 85%) of these children were low income. No study up to this time had ever assessed the direct effect of foundational skills knowledge on state assessments.

So what was the outcome of the reading wars? What did most schools and reading programs do? Stay tuned, but before you do, collect your thoughts.

Stop and Think

What do you see as the most important parts of this chapter so far?

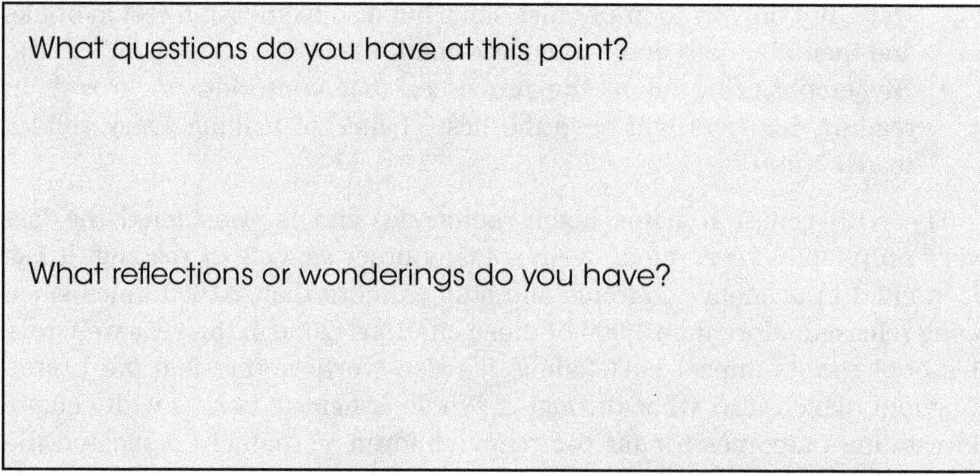

What Was the Outcome of the Reading Wars?

The Literacy Community responded in what seemed like a very common-sense, flexible, practical, and child-oriented solution by taking the report at its word (*to create a balanced reading program*) by combining the best principles of phonics and Whole Language. This soon came to be called Balanced Literacy: a balance between phonics and a skills-oriented approach to mastering some parts of reading and a Whole Language or more holistic approach. It seemed like the perfect marriage.

Although there is not one universally accepted definition of balanced literacy, there has come to be widely accepted agreement on its components: It typically includes some combination of interactive read-aloud, shared, or whole-class reading, guided reading (almost always done in small groups by ability), writing workshop (where the stages of writing from brainstorming through editing are the emphasis), free-choice independent reading, word study (phonics in some cases or it could include morphology, vocabulary, grammar, and spelling), the use of authentic text, and lots of instruction in comprehension strategies through minilessons. What could possibly go wrong?

Given the broad range of classroom ingredients that are understood as part and parcel of balanced reading, it has been challenging for researchers to conduct any definitive research on balanced literacy as an approach. This is because of how many different ways it can be done and how little agreement there is on what, exactly, is the balance. What is clear from even a casual perusal of reading programs or journals that focus on elementary reading is that balanced literacy has been the dominant form of instruction in elementary schools since shortly after the NRP report was released in 2000. What is also clear is it has not moved the needle nearly enough on the scores of low-income children, children of color, or children coming into our schools with a home language other than English (English-language learners). That is the story no matter what ELA or reading assessment you look at.

Clearly, this great armistice in the Reading Wars has failed to date to support the reading attainment of the children who depend on school to help them the most.

Why hasn't it?

The NPR's research report was not about phonics: it was about *systematic* phonics. Go back and look at those curated quotes (the first set of bulleted quotes in this chapter). They don't reference phonics. They reference *systematic* phonics approaches. Each time. The report asserts best practice for teaching decoding is to "use a planned, sequential introduction of a set of phonic elements along with teaching and practice of those elements." Further, "though differences exist, the hallmark of systematic phonics programs is that they delineate a planned, sequential set of phonic elements and they teach these elements explicitly and systematically." And it went on, "having children read text that provides practice using these relations to decode words," as opposed to, "Instruction lacking an emphasis on phonics instruction does not teach letter-sound relations systematically and selects text for children according to other principles." "The purpose of this report is to examine the research evidence concerning systematic phonics instruction" compared with "the performance of children given no systematic phonics or no phonics instruction."

The report goes on to note that "systematic phonics instruction typically involves explicitly teaching children a pre-specified set of letter-sound relations and having children read text that provides practice using these relations to decode words. Instruction lacking an emphasis on phonics instruction does not teach letter-sound relations systematically and selects text for children according to other principles. The latter form of instruction includes Whole Word programs, Whole Language programs, and some basal reader programs."

In sum—and this is really important—the report of the National Reading Panel *only* looked at systematic phonics approaches and compared them with approaches that were either not systematic or did no phonics at all.

In sum—and this is really important—the report of the National Reading Panel only *looked at systematic phonics approaches and compared them with approaches that were either not systematic or did no phonics at all.*

Balanced literacy has a really loose set of defining features and no agreed-upon standard of practice. The balance is all in the eye of the beholder. In no classroom we have been in, in no materials marketed[3] as balanced literacy we have reviewed, have we found systematic phonics as defined by the NRP. In balanced literacy settings, children and their teachers aren't using materials that follow a scope and sequence of phonics patterns, explicitly and transparently teach those patterns, or encourage reading books early in their reading journeys designed to support learning those patterns in a rock-solid way.

As scores of low-income children and students of color stayed flat and pressure mounted, we have seen many schools and districts purchase stand-alone phonics programs. They generally do provide a scope and sequence and are designed for explicit teaching. So they should be a step toward a more systematic approach. But they get sabotaged in execution. These same districts and schools recommend spending very little time on the explicit teaching and student practice of phonics patterns, often as little as 10–15 minutes a day, even in first grade. The stand-alone programs do not always provide phonics readers (shockingly, even many basal reading publishers don't have the phonics readers as part of their basic package, so sometimes districts don't buy them). So teachers use what they have, which are either the supplemental leveled readers or a school-based variation designed to work in those leveled reading groups for skills instruction and guided reading.

Leveled readers are not organized by phonics patterns, so it is random whether or not they will provide words that use the phonics patterns being taught in the sequence. Early leveled readers are designed to support readers using their knowledge of sight words (words introduced and practiced as wholes, not as the sounds that make up them) and words cued by the picture, sentence syntax, or the teacher. Balanced literacy advocates that readers use the "three-cueing system" to recognize words based on the idea that children recognize words by a combination of context or meaning, syntax, and visual (referred to as M, S, and V). Visual is often called graphophonemic (maybe to avoid even using the word "phonics"?). The three-cueing system makes complete sense intuitively, but there is no research supporting it as the best mechanism to recognize words. There is much research, however, showing that proficient readers do not use the three-cueing system and weaker readers do. As weaker readers often cannot decode using their phonetic knowledge, they are forced to rely on syntax and context, which will fail them at increasing rates as texts' complexity increases. For an in-depth look at the history and misunderstandings of the three-cueing system, there is a long piece by Marilyn Adams included in this chapter's resources.

Let's look more closely at a leveled reader compared with a decodable by

[3] The big publishers offer comprehensive ELA programs ("basals") that do offer a systematic phonics sequence and comprehensive foundational skills programs. Some have phonics readers, but some of those are sold as supplemental material! They all have non–decodable leveled readers as part of their core for students, and many teachers, in our experience, default to these right away. Importantly, the sheer volume of stuff in these programs is overwhelming, so teachers don't tend to do the full foundational skills program. They don't feel they have time.

My aunt goes to the store.
She goes on a bus.

8

My uncle goes to his office.
He goes on a ferry boat.

9

FIGURE 5. Leveled text sample. From *Getting around the City* Reading A-Z (Level D) late kindergarten. Used by permission.

looking at a couple pages from each type of reader. Figure 5 shows two pages from a mid-to-late kindergarten leveled reader[4] followed by two pages of a decodable reader (Figure 6) for about the same time of the year.

Let's start with the decodable reader.

Decodables are designed to have most of the words in them contain phonics patterns that are being taught or were taught already. All the high-frequency words in it have already been introduced and learned to the point where they can be recognized as whole words. In *Josh's New Home*, the following phonics patterns will have all been taught to children: all five short-vowel sounds and basic consonants needed to create simple CV or CVC words, the /ch/ and /sh/ digraphs, and the high-frequency words *and*, *the*, and *a*. Children would be looking at words and sound–spelling patterns they had been directly taught but getting to experience them through reading (decoding) meaningful text on their own or with a friend.

Decodable readers are how some publishers and educators responded to the NRP research findings that asserted that part of systematic phonics is "having children read text that provides practice using these [phonetic] relations to decode words." Clearly, a decodable does this. A systematic phonics program using decodables will teach most or all of the phonics patterns needed to recognize words explicitly through lessons and then let children practice and experience those patterns through these books, games, puzzles, riddles, and other activities (how to teach a systematic, structured phonics program is the topic of the next chapter). The decodables will have multiple examples of the phonics pattern or patterns that are being taught explicitly in that week or unit. They'll also include words with the phonics patterns already learned. So

[4] Learning A-Z kindly allowed us to use this older sample of one of their leveled reading books. LA-Z is also a good, low-cost source of phonics readers and other supports for teaching systematic phonics, as we will discuss in the next chapter.

Josh and Ben sit and chat in the den

Josh fed Ben a nut and jam

FIGURE 6. Decodable text sample. From *Josh's New Home*. Kindergarten Reading Foundations Skills Block by EL Education (https://curriculum.eleducation.org/). Used under CC BY 4.0 (https://creativecommons.org/licenses/by/4.0/legalcode).

children are *always* getting to see and use what they've been taught whenever they read any decodable. The decodable reader lets the students put what they've been taught to immediate use, reinforcing the purpose of studying the phonics pattern as a tool for reading.[5]

This careful teaching and practicing of specific sound–spelling patterns are repeated through all the phonic patterns. This is how a systematic phonics program teaches word recognition going all the way through the patterns in English.

Along the way, some programs will expose students to the morphology of the English language. Although morphology is not generally considered part of foundational skills, it's really important. (Morphology is the study of the smallest unit of letters that convey meaning—which is how words are frequently built in English. There's an article linked at the end of this chapter that discusses in depth why morphology is important for children's vocabulary growth and learning, as well as why it is morphology that makes English spelling make sense.)

Now let's look at the leveled reader.

In these two pages, you have words that contain one or more examples of the following phonics patterns: In the first sentence, there is 'y' as a /ī/ sound

[5] It's important to stop and note that we aren't arguing decodables are all that children should be reading! They need exposure to all sorts of books and print, both read to them in rich interactions and available to read on their own. But our focus here is on teaching children to read, so we aren't talking about the *rest* of an ideal ELA program for young children. Next book!

in *My*, the vowel diphthong 'au' in *aunt*, and 'o' as a long vowel /ō/ in *goes*; also in *goes* there is an 'es' plural, **and** 's' at the end of *goes* is making a 'z' sound, not an 's' sound. The sentence ends with *store*, containing the consonant blend 'st' and the 'r'-controlled 'o.' In the next sentence, the reader encounters *she*, usually a sight word or formed by the digraph 'sh' followed by an unusual e making the /ē/ sound at the end of a word, then sees *goes* again before seeing the first CVC word in *bus*. Tired yet? There's another page!

On the second page, the two sentence pattern continues (as it has since the second page of the book). But now the reader sees the /ŭ/ (VC) as well as the –cle pattern in *uncle* before seeing the same sight words as before plus *his*, another sight word. But then comes *office*, a phonetically irregular word. The next sentence has both *ferry* and *boat*. In *ferry*, the 'y' at the end is now making a /ē/ sound, and you have not an 'r'-controlled vowel, but this time the 'e' isn't 'r' controlled. *Boat* has a digraph oa, which makes the /ō/ sound. The two sentences contain the high-frequency words *she*, *to*, *the*, *on*, *his*, and *a*.

It is extremely unlikely that a kindergartener would have been taught each of the sound-spelling patterns and sight words needed to be successful in decoding this text. Children probably can't read this book by applying whatever phonics patterns they've been shown by late kindergarten. The practice opportunity is not there. Instead, children would read this book by memorizing the repeating sentence pattern, using their knowledge of sight words, and then guessing at the nouns from the picture clues, or, as in *uncle*, getting the information from the context of having just read about something the aunt did. Alternately, the teacher might read the book aloud with the children following, and then the children would read the book on their own, perhaps after a few chorale readings. During these exposures, it is assumed the students would pick up the phonics patterns inside the words they were reading. But what if they don't?

So, in a leveled reading program, where leveled books are the bread-and-butter reading materials and decodable readers aren't part of the classroom, how do children learn all of the phonics patterns they need to build a solid reading foundation? Hundreds of thousands of children manage to.

First of all, some phonics patterns will be pointed out and discussed by the teacher as children work with the leveled reader. If there is any phonics instruction at all in the class (and it is rare that phonics is ignored altogether), then the teacher is likely to point out the patterns recently introduced or to remind children that they have been taught a pattern in a word they aren't reading correctly. The idea is that children will recognize these in the current leveled reader and then in any text thereafter. But clearly, even in these two pages from *Getting around the City*, there are far more things going on that a teacher could or should point out to reinforce all the sound–spelling patterns that students need. Children would be bewildered. A teacher simply can't point out all the untaught phonics patterns in a leveled reader, even a fairly low-level one like our Level D book.

For the phonics patterns not pointed out, the expectation is that children will infer the pattern or guess at the word from the picture clues and the sentence pattern. They will, for example, see *goes* and hear the final 'z' sound and infer that 's' at the end of some words can make a 'z' sound. Then they'll read *bus* and think "Oops! It seems like 's' must make different sounds sometimes!" Similarly, they would see and hear *store*, notice that another word they know, *or* is inside it, and figure out that 'or' always sounds like or, even inside words. More commonly, the expectation is that one of two things should happen: there are enough clues between the pictures and the other words for young readers to figure out what some words are (even if they contain unknown patterns), or children are so familiar with a concept, the unknown word will come to them. For example, that could perhaps be the case for *aunt* and *uncle*. Though they both represent fairly advanced phonics patterns, children could either figure them out from context or have heard and read enough stories with relatives in them to commit those two words to memory after seeing them a number of times. Same with *ferry boat*. It's certainly more likely that children who know about ferry boats will guess both words correctly.

Many children do learn to read in balanced literacy classrooms. Why does this kind of "light touch" teaching work well for some children to learn to read and not others? What is true about children this kind of instruction and exposure work well for?

The chart on the following page lays out what lots of studies and our own experiences tell us are the critical factors for whether or not children will thrive within a balanced literacy structure when they're in the primary grades and learning to read. Although these are generalities and there are always exceptions, these factors still hold. We've placed an asterisk (*) with items we think are the most important of all. It's also important to understand these are a cluster of constructs. Any one of them can interact with any others. For example, even a child who is read to frequently and hears lots of talk about letters and sounds might still require more explicit instruction and more chances to practice. So discussions of letters and letter sounds might not seem to support this student as much because he just needs more exposures.

We aren't assigning motivation or judgment to the factors laid out in the chart you just read. We had our own mix of them present in our own household and have seen endless variations among the many students we've worked with over long careers. Many of the factors listed are by-products of the way many of us live, which is invariably with too little time and too many demands on our attention. We've yet to meet the parent who didn't want the best for her or his child. We've known best the two children, now grown men, we raised, and then the children of the Family Academy. Those are the experiences

BALANCED LITERACY (BL) APPROACH

Tends to Work for Children Who:	Doesn't Tend to Work for Children Who:
• Are read to more ▫ When read to, get lots of talk about letters and letter sounds as part of the experience	• Are read to less ▫ Hear less discussion of letters and letter sounds when read aloud to
• Have caregivers who frequently and clearly signal the importance of reading and have lots of books around the home	• Have caregivers who signal the importance of reading less clearly and/or less often and have less books around the home
• Spend lots of time pretend-reading books, including picture books; tend to reread favorites multiple times ▫ Attended preschools that exposed them to phonological awareness (including phonemic awareness) and early reading activities	• Spend less time or no time pretend-reading books, including picture books ▫ Didn't attend preschools that exposed them to phonological awareness (including phonemic awareness) and early reading activities
• Have a wider and larger range of general knowledge (whether acquired from books, media, preschool, or experiences)	• Have a smaller, more narrow range of general knowledge (whether acquired from books, media, preschool, or experiences)
• Possess a larger, wide-ranging vocabulary, including a base of Tier 2 vocabulary	• Possess a smaller, more narrow vocabulary, along with fewer Tier 2 words
• Spend less time on screens	• Spend more time on screens
• Get frequent enrichment opportunities and/or access to tutoring as needed ▫ Need less explicit instruction and supported practice to learn to decode	• Get fewer enrichment opportunities and/or don't have access to tutoring if the need arises ▫ Require more (or far more) explicit instruction and supported practice to learn to decode

we draw on for the stories and lessons in this book. But it's important to note again that the ingredients of that chart are also borne out by many reading research studies. They probably resonate with your own experiences.

At the Family Academy, as we mentioned earlier, we were all in on being a Whole Language school for our first two years. As you know, that got us the lowest reading scores in New York City. Only *one* child in our first group was reading in second grade, and she was taught to read by her no-nonsense mother, not by us. We changed to a systematic phonics program, scrambled to remediate our entire first group of children so as not to sabotage their entire education, and improved scores dramatically, just as happened in the schools and for the teachers whose data were shown by that Paige study we discussed (with the 31 lowest-scoring schools in the poorest-performing district in the state).

We kept all the read-aloud. We always had lots of rich discussions, and we provided lots of enrichment within the school day and year. We went on many trips, and we built knowledge through a rich science and social studies curriculum we dubbed our general knowledge curriculum, which was built around lots of reading, as well as hands-on experiences. All those changes were important. But what turned us around was making sure every child had a robust, systematic, and structured foundational skills experience for as long as they needed.

In the next chapter, we'll describe how we did it, what the research says is the best practice in phonics, and how you can bring systematic phonics into your classroom, whether it is a balanced literacy setting or something else.

But before you go on, stop and reflect.

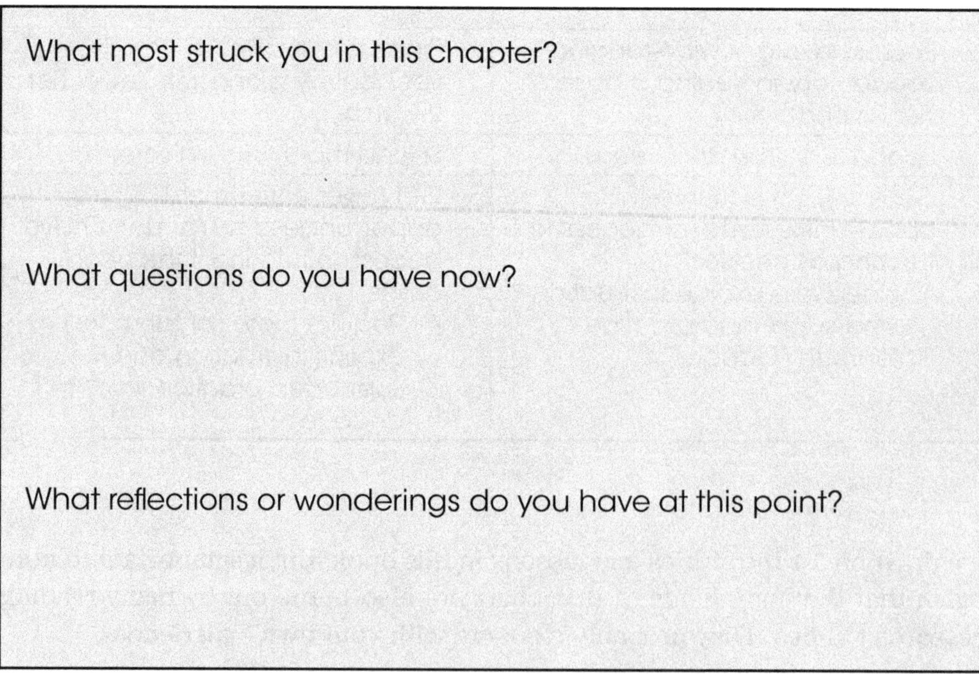

Sources for Deeper Learning and Teaching

A short, clear article on the Three-Cueing System and what is wrong with how it's been put into practice

http://www.balancedreading.com/3cue.html

An in-depth but readable look at the history and misunderstandings of the three-cueing system by Marilyn Adams

http://www.balancedreading.com/3cue-adams.html

For more on how directly teaching both phonics and morphology will strengthen children's ability to make sense of English

https://www.ldatschool.ca/phonological-morphological-approaches/

A link to Head Start's School Readiness Effective Practice Guides

https://eclkc.ohs.acf.hhs.gov/school-readiness/effective-practice-guides/introduction

Works Consulted

Association of the Masters of the Boston Public Schools. (1844). *Remarks on the Seventh Annual Report of the Hon. Horace Mann, Secretary of the Massachusetts Board of Education.* Boston, MA: C. C. Little and J. Brown.

Brown, M. C., Sibley, D. E., Washington, J. A., Rogers, T. T., Edwards, J. R., MacDonald, M. C., & Seidenberg, M. S. (2015). Impact of dialect use on a basic component of learning to read. *Frontiers in Psychology, 6*, 196. doi:10.3389/fpsyg.2015.00196

California leads revival of teaching by phonics. *The New York Times.* (1996, May 22). Retrieved from https://www.nytimes.com/1996/05/22/us/california-leads-revival-of-teaching-by-phonics.html

Gray, W., & May, A. (1968). *We come and go.* New York, NY: Grosset and Dunlap/Penguin.

National Reading Panel (US), National Institute of Child Health, & Human Development (US). (2000). *Report of the national reading panel: Teaching children to read: An evidence-based assessment of the scientific research literature on reading and its implications for reading instruction: Reports of the subgroups.* Bethesda, MD: National Institute of Child Health and Human Development, National Institutes of Health.

Paige, D. D., Smith, G. S., Rasinski, T.V., Rupley, W. H., Magpuri-Lavell, T., & Nichols, W. D. (2018). A path analytic model linking foundational skills to grade 3 state reading achievement. *The Journal of Educational Research*, 1–11. doi:10.1080/00220671.2018.1445609

Stanovich, K. E. (2009). Matthew effects in reading: Some consequences of individual differences in the acquisition of literacy. *Journal of Education, 189*, 23–55. doi: 10.1177/0022057409189001-204

Yatvin, J. (2000). Minority view. In *Report of the National Reading Panel.* Bethesda, MD: National Institute of Child Health and Development.

Chapter Five

How to Teach Systematic Phonics: A Story

When new students came into the school in the early years, David liked to spend time in the classroom with them and the child assigned to them as a guide to life at the Family Academy. This is his story. Tyrone came in to the school in mid-November of first grade. Gregory had been assigned to be his guide. Tyrone had a great smile, beautiful deep-set brown eyes, and a ton of personality. According to his mother, he came from the "loose-interpretation school" as far as rules were concerned and pretty much lived his life that way. Tyrone looked every minute of the day as if he were about to leap to the front of the class with a mic in his hand and start entertaining. He had lots of charm, but you needed to keep an eye on him! Gregory's approach to rules and life was as rigid as Tyrone's was loose. Follow the letter of the law, head down, do your work. Don't get into trouble. I'm sure if you asked Gregory if he would rather come to the front of the room to tell a story or go to the dentist, he'd pick the dentist. No need to keep a watchful eye on Gregory. It was not an accident that Gregory was chosen to help orient Tyrone to life at the Family Academy. That included the reading block.

"You can't read these books! There's not enough pictures! Besides, the teacher is supposed to help you know what's going on! And where are the pictures anyway? This is wack!" (Mid-1990s Harlem for "this makes no sense.") This, more or less, was Tyrone's first response to reading at the Family Academy. Gregory turned, faced him, dropped his new glasses over his nose, and gave him a look that could only be interpreted along the lines of, "What hath God wrought!?" But Gregory's assignment was Tyrone, and he took his responsibilities very seriously. Gregory began to explain that his group was working on the /ŭ/ sound and the letter that stands for that sound. He then showed Tyrone the words in the lessons that had this phonics pattern and read them as Tyrone looked on. It takes smarts to be a comedian, and no sooner did Tyrone grasp the pattern than he asked what was going on with the other words; what sounds did they make? The methodical Gregory went right back to the earlier decodable booklets and the first parts of the practice book and began to show Tyrone "how it all worked," as he said. The teacher soon came over with her plan for Tyrone, part of which did include Gregory's helping him catch up.

What was interesting and gratifying about this was that Gregory knew there was a system to learning how to read, a record of sorts in the workbook and the decodable. It all made sense, and he could actually help his charge. Tyrone, a much quicker (though not necessarily deeper) learner, realized this almost immediately, yet he had learned very little about reading before he came to us.

We think this is a great part of why systematic phonics is so powerful and why the National Reading Panel (NRP) did not recommend merely phonics but systematic phonics. For Gregory, the system made sense, he knew what to do to the point that he could explain it to another first-grader who didn't. Tyrone, just as smart and much quicker, didn't learn much about literacy in the school he came from. Having little experience with books, words, stories, letters, or the idea that letters represent sounds, he didn't see the big picture. So he said to Gregory at the end of that first lesson, "I never thought about any of this, I just tried to memorize the words."

The NRP, toward the conclusion of its review of the literature on phonics, noted that "Although differences exist, the hallmark of systematic phonics programs is that they delineate a planned, sequential set of phonic elements and they teach these elements explicitly and systematically" (NRP, 2-89). To start off, we'll look at what is meant by a "sequential set of phonic elements," otherwise known as a scope and sequence. We'll then go on to discuss important aspects of teaching these "explicitly and systematically." We hope to convince you of the importance of these factors for children's reading health, so you go out and get what you need to make sure it happens for the children in your setting. We can't provide you with all the details you'd need to know exactly what to do. A good program can. So we'll look at some of the best examples of the resources we know.

A study led by Heidi Mesmer, a well-respected reading researcher, noted that five years after the NRP, if teachers reported doing systematic phonics, they included a scope and sequence in their definition (Mesmer & Griffith, 2005). So it makes sense to start with scope and sequence, just as Gregory instinctively did with Tyrone.

Nearly all foundational skills scope and sequences since roughly the mid-1980s start with phonological awareness, just as we did at the Family Academy, although they differ on how much time and attention they recommend be given to this area of instruction. All the basals now begin here as well although we have found the big commercial basal programs to be generally weak in this area and short on the fun factor overall. As you remember, we recommend Marilyn Adam's book, *Phonemic Awareness in Young Children*, if you don't feel your materials do a good job with phonemic and phonological awareness. The Adams book does.

Before going onto phonics, many scope and sequences provide a diagnostic assessment to determine what the children in your class already know.

This will help you with planning and with grouping your children appropriately. You may already have a good assessment instrument in place in your district that accompanies your materials. We recommend *Word Journeys* (see the resources section at the end of the chapter) as a good all-in-one tool if you don't.

Many scope and sequences teach letter naming concurrently with phonological awareness, others start with phonological awareness in isolation and add letter naming later. A 1999 meta-study (meta-studies are studies that review all of the studies for a given topic; in other words "studies of studies") showed that combining phonemic awareness with letter training was more effective than phonological awareness alone (Bus & IJzendoorn, 1999). Because phonemic awareness and early letter–sound understanding mirror each other, folding both into instruction quickens learning. So you should feel free to combine them, even if your current materials don't.

From here all scope and sequences go on to phonics. They tend to start with initial and final consonants, short vowels, and then long vowels. They generally move on to digraphs (two or more letters representing one sound as in "ch," "sh," and "ph" for consonants and "ea," "ai," and "eigh" for vowels, etc.), 'r'-controlled vowels (the vowel sounds in *barn*, *fern*, and *bird*), and diphthongs (two letters make a sound different from either one's primary sound "oi" as in *boil*, "ou" as in *bound*). Some sequences will then go into more uncommon vowel combinations, inflections, tenses, and how to break apart multisyllabic words. We know of no research showing one scope and sequence is better than others, so you should feel confident using the one you have available to you.

There are several scope and sequences in the resources section at the end of the chapter. We've included short descriptions of how they're organized, and they are all available online. We think it's worth your taking a look at these to get a sense of the nature of some different scope and sequences, especially if you aren't familiar with phonics programs.

Once you have a scope and sequence you feel good about, the next step is to "teach these elements explicitly and systematically" (NRP, 2-89), just as Gregory started to do. This means providing students with lessons that introduce and teach each of the phonics patterns in the scope and sequence through direct instruction, examples, and active practice opportunities. The goal is always to learn the pattern and cement it in memory through games, songs, poems, and riddles or regular ol' written practice work in rich combination. There is an endless variety of possible activities for teaching phonics patterns. If you're using a good program, or if you adopt one because we've persuaded you systematic phonics is crucial, it should contain everything you and your children need. It should also be fun. We've discussed the comprehensive English Language Arts (ELA) programs that do an especially good job with foundational skills in the appendix and have included some good-quality free resources for teaching foundational reading in the resources section at the end of this chapter.

Lessons and activities in systematic phonics programs introduce the patterns in isolation at first so children can focus on the sound–symbol connection. When they see the patterns in words, that experience, too, is almost always out of the context of reading a book or short passage at first.

This practice is where much of the fuel heaped on the battlefields of the Reading Wars comes from. As you'll remember from the last chapter, much of the controversy in the Whole Language versus Phonics focused on whole language enthusiasts' belief that reading instruction should *only and always* be in context, meaning phonics patterns should be reinforced by being encountered in books students are reading and that should be enough to solidify that pattern and for students to intuit the connection.

That is why *some* Whole Language advocates rightly claimed there were phonics in Whole Language and many advocates of Balanced Literacy now rightly claim there is phonics in Balanced Literacy as well. And there were and are. But Balanced Literacy programs seldom spend enough time examining phonics patterns closely so children can understand how they work, nor do they tend to offer sufficient practice opportunities out of context. Also, there is not generally a strict scope and sequence, so there is no guarantee every pattern would be directly taught. Some would be left to be inferred. As we discussed in the last chapter, that leaves too many children without the focus and time many of them need to master the patterns. If you're still reading at this point, we're going to assume you're with us on this and forge ahead.

We can't give you examples of lessons for every phonics pattern you'd encounter in a scope and sequence, of course. One of the strengths of systematic phonics is that the same types of introductory lessons and practice activities can be used for almost any phonics pattern. Ritualizing the lessons in this way makes it easier and more productive for students and teachers. We'll use the /ĕ/ pattern as an example. In this example, we'll highlight how a lesson that is part of a systematic phonics program would differ from one that is not.

Often lessons begin with a phonemic awareness warm-up using the phonics pattern that is the focus of the lesson. This serves a number of purposes. Students start to warm up their phonemic "muscles" and think about sounds in words as a prelude to thinking about the letters or combination of letters that represent those sounds. These kinds of lessons have been done by the children before, and they're likely to be good at it, so a quick warm-up builds confidence for what is to come. And of course it's fun, and fun is good! These activities can be done whole class or in groups, should move fast and feel snappy, and take just 3–5 minutes.

Phonemic Awareness Warm-Up for /ĕ/ in First Grade

Do the following chorally with the group you're working with.

- Teachers asks students to combine the /b/, /e/, and /t/ sounds. What do you get? (bet)
  (As you'll remember from the Phonemic Awareness chapter, we need to be *really* careful not to add a vowel sound after the /b/ [don't say /buh/]. The best way we know to do this is to exhale before you say individual phonemes. The vowels ride in on your breath, so if you're out of breath when you say consonant sounds, you'll pronounce them cleanly. (Just like your students, you'll get good with practice!)[1]
- Take away the /b/ sound and what do you get? (et)
- What's a word that rhymes with egg, most people have two of them to stand on? (leg)
- What is it called when you hear the same sound repeated from somewhere else? It begins with the /e/ sound. Then ask students to, "Turn to your partner and while going up and down in place, say 'echo' in an echo of each other. Echo begins with /e/."
- How many sounds in "tell"? What's the first sound, the second, and the last?
- Turn to your partner and see how many words you can come up with that rhyme with "tell."

Introductory Phonics Lesson for /ĕ/

Next comes the full phonics lesson with /ĕ/. There are lots of ways to do this teaching, and this is just a sample. We believe, so we keep emphasizing, that you should have a good foundational reading program that has good activities and materials—one you believe in—and you should follow it.

We're using a chart to walk you through the rest of the lesson. On the left are the teacher moves or the student practice opportunities. On the right is our commentary about the role that aspect of the lesson plays to reinforce learning.

---

[1] Search for "44 Phonemes" on YouTube for the best video we've seen on precise pronunciation. It's from Rollins University, and it's only 5 minutes long. The camera focuses on the woman's mouth as she pronounces precisely and gives good tips along the way. You can search YouTube for "pronouncing phonemes."

Teacher and Student Actions	Notes and Explanation
Today we're going to work with the short 'e' sound that you've just been playing with, but now, as always, we're going to move to writing and reading words with these sounds. We're moving from phonemes to phonics!	Because this is done every day, some teachers invent a transition song with lyrics like, "We're moving from phonemes to phonics" (3 times) repeated with the final line, "And we do it every day!" to the tune of "The Farmer in the Dell." If that's too goofy for you, make your own ritual. We're pretty big on "goofy" elements in foundational reading, especially when it gets everybody singing and moving.
I'm going to read *Horton Hatches the Egg* to you, but Horton is going to have a new name today. You get to lift your arms every time you hear a word that has the short 'e' in it. I'm going to write each short 'e' words you found on the board so everybody can see it. Then we're going to underline the letter that represented the sound. Remember, we're working with the short 'e' sound. 'E' as in *egg*.	There are *many* ways to introduce the new pattern. One of our favorites is with a fun book, being sure, however, that the book has already been read multiple times for understanding and appreciation. *Recipe for Reading,* one of the scope and sequences mentioned in the back, suggested Dr. Seuss's *Horton Hatches the Egg* but substituting "Ed" for "Horton." You're also generating a list of short 'e' words you'll use later in the lesson.
Now we're going to make it more challenging! You've got the short 'e' words down. Remember our words like map and cat? We're going to listen for those in the next few pages of "Ed" *Hatches the Egg*.	Once you see students responding quickly and accurately, you can add another phonics pattern that has already been learned, maybe another short vowel sound or an initial consonant. This is more difficult but serves the purpose of review and definitely grows students' careful listening ability. Because you're working in a systematic phonics program, you know what's been learned already. More importantly, you know what patterns would benefit from more review.

Continued on next page

Teacher and Student Actions	Notes and Explanation
Nice job on the book! We're going to go back to our short 'e' word list we made. Remember? We have Ed and egg and other words on it? I'm going to read those words with you (some of you will read them, too). You're going to practice blending those words from the list by using your fingers the way we were doing last week with the short 'a' words. I'll show you again with *egg*. I'll tap and say each sound, and then I'll point to each letter that makes a sound while you tap. Point to each word and say it. Model this each time facing the children and watch carefully while they "blend" with their fingers and say the sounds too. Watch to make sure children are able to hear the sounds and blend them for each word.	Expeditionary Learning Education and Core Knowledge Language Arts (core ELA programs mentioned at chapter's end and described in the appendix on good ELA programs) both use a thumb-to-finger tapping technique to represent the sounds in the words. The thumb moves from the viewers' left to right, tapping fingers to represent the sounds heard in the word. Be careful modeling this so what the children see is your thumb moving from left to right! For example, for the word *egg*, students would tap two of their fingers with their thumb. For *met*, the thumb would tap three fingers. Children can also use tiles or small blocks or math manipulatives and touch as many objects as they hear sounds. They are now associating sounds with the written representation of them.
Now you're going to write some of the short 'e' words we've been working with. We'll do it one word at a time. One of you will come up and write each word on the board so we can all see what it looks like together. You ready?	Next comes the opportunity for children to practice writing this new pattern for themselves. Whiteboards are ideal for this because they're so flexible and you can easily monitor for children's progress before they erase and write the next word.

Other Active Ways to Reinforce and Solidify Phonics Learning and More Explanation

- A good intermediate activity between finger tapping to blend the words and writing them on whiteboards or paper is to have students "air write" the word containing /ĕ/ while the teacher or a student volunteer writes the same word on the board. Sometimes called "sky writing," the entire arm can be engaged in making big, sweeping letters if you have enough space to do so without students whacking each other. If not, have them write just with their fingers or even trace the word with one finger into the palm of their other hand. This is good to do before students write on paper or whiteboard.

- Remember, the NRP is clear about the role of "systematic and explicit" practice for each phonics pattern in the scope and sequence. The next activities provide more practice repetitions and can be done in centers, small groups, or whole class. Again, the sky is the limit on your creativity with designing practice opportunities. We've included mostly inexpensive, low-tech practice ideas, but this is an area where computer games and programs are excellent (and motivating) ways to get good phonics practice in.

- Flash cards are an inexpensive staple (index cards make perfect flashcards) and can be used in a variety of ways. One of the simplest is for you or a student group leader to have a deck of cards for the patterns already studied and currently being learned. Cards are held up one at a time while the students read the word chorally. The eventual goal within each session is to recognize and say the word as fast as possible to build toward automaticity of decoding with that pattern. Don't rush this because children, as you know, need varying amounts of repetition before they can achieve automaticity, but pay attention to how your students are doing and encourage as much speed as they can manage each time.

- Proficient readers will eventually recognize words in about a quarter of a second. Proficient decoding clearly requires accuracy as well as speed (automaticity). We'll discuss this much more in the next chapter on fluency, but this is the first-grade version of that at the single-word level.
- You can put some adrenalin into flash card work if children each have their own deck of words (on index cards). They can make their own as part of their spelling and writing practice. They start with the deck of cards straight down, the leader (this position would rotate if not the teacher) picks up one of her cards and reads the word aloud, then the children hunt for that word and hold the card up when they find it. Whoever finds the right card and reads it aloud correctly first wins and gets to control the next round. There is research (McGaugh, 2006) showing that this type of adrenalin rush enhances memory formations. American Reading Company Core Reading, one of the ELA programs in the appendix, has many of these types of activities.

- "Flash Card Baseball" is a variation on this. Here, one child is the "pitcher" and reads the word aloud to the team that's "up to bat." If the batter finds the right card and reads it, she goes to first base and the next batter comes up and so on. If a child says she's ready to "call a home run," she gets a wildcard from another deck that has words with phonics patterns not yet learned. If she reads the word right, that's a home run; if not she's out. There are dozens of ways that flashcards can be used for practice that are fun and develop accuracy and automaticity of word recognition.

- Word Sorts are popular and good. In this case, the teacher or leader would read a word with either the /ĕ/ sound or one of the other short vowel sounds that has already been learned. Children then write the word on paper in the column labeled with the appropriate short vowel sound.

- Precision Phonics Dancing is a great example of active practice we saw in a school in Nashville, Tennessee. The teacher divided the class in half and had everyone line up across from each other. She would read out a word, and the children in line would take as many "troll steps" forward as there were sounds in the word while saying a sound per step. They said the whole word at their stop point. Then they returned to their sides while saying each letter that spelled that word as they stomped back to their places. Once they were back to their starting point, they would once again say the word.

Some Additional Important Points about Practice Activities

- Many teachers report that using the same daily routines each time they introduce a new phonics patterns saves time and preparation. Children enjoy the sense of ritual, the comfort of repeating familiar patterns, and the independence doing so yields.
- It makes sense that learning is enhanced if children move and use their bodies as much as possible. Muscle movement not only engages the child but has proven to be effective in approaches such as Orton-Gillingham, a well-established program for children with reading disabilities. It used to be thought that multisensory methods such as these were only needed for students with dyslexia, but we know now that it enhances learning for everyone. It's also a lot more fun to move your body instead of sitting still all the time.
- Practice activities mean students are *always* reviewing past learnings. As you saw in the activities just discussed, children have to recognize the word and work to spell it, putting their sound–symbol learning to use each time. Although it is true that every phonics pattern learned (as well as many others, as yet unlearned) will appear in the pages of a leveled reader and can be observed, there's a big difference in the type of focus we're describing here. In the leveled reader, children have lots of other assists. They can use pictures, syntax, context, or repetition patterns to name the word. Thus, they *do not have to focus as much on the qualities of the word.* When you *only* have the word, you are much more likely to focus on the word itself. That makes you much more likely to learn

the phonics pattern than when you have all the other supports a text can provide. This makes sense and was confirmed in a well-done study (Landi, Perfetti, Bolger, Dunlap, & Foorman, 2006). The scientists who ran the study get the punchline here. They concluded that words are *read* better in context but *learned* better out of context. Because our goal is for all children to be able to decode automatically and effortlessly, the way competent readers do, we need for them to learn all those patterns solidly. Out-of-context word study has a vital role to play in decoding.

- The Shaywitzes (a husband-and-wife team of research psychiatrists who have done groundbreaking work on the brain and reading) used functional magnetic resonance imaging (fMRIs) in their work. These are pictures of the brain while it's engaging in a specific task. They scanned weak readers while they were reading. They repeated the scan after the students had engaged in a systematic phonics program to remediate their gaps. They found the neural pathways in the part of the brain where reading resides were actually thicker and stronger after the systematic phonics work! They note this benefit is essentially an effect of practice. We can't imagine more concrete proof for the effectiveness of systematic phonics or the importance of practice than brains literally getting stronger.
- Practice is essential for children to bind phonics patterns permanently into long-term memory so that words can be read accurately and automatically.
- We know students who enter kindergarten more comfortable with books and words understand the alphabetic principle, have some phonemic awareness, have been read to thousands of times or more, and are used to making inferences may need very little practice before they have patterns locked into long-term memory.
- Conversely, some students move more slowly than others, some a lot more slowly. What is behind this pattern is a differentiated need for practice. Systematic phonics is organized to *easily* provide more practice for those who need more or less for those who don't. In every case, practice is cumulative. It continually reinforces the previously introduced patterns until they are solidly entered into long-term working memory and can be retrieved automatically. We always taught foundational skills in differentiated groups at Family Academy so children could have as much or as little time as they needed to progress.
- What about those students who need not just practice but *far* more practice? More than what they get in group work, more than teachers can provide, possibly more than there is time for in the course of the school day? We recommend the use of workbooks. In our experience, most

children enjoy the clarity and focus they provide. Workbooks are ideal for practice for those students who need more. At the Family Academy, we used *Explode the Code*, from Educators Publishing Service, which had six pages of practice for every phonics pattern. For children who needed more, there were extra "half-step" books that had that many more pages of practice again for each of the same patterns introduced in the book before, with different activities.

- Our Family Academy students generally did well with the workbooks and liked them. But they did better with them in some classes than others, and we started to see the differences showing up in learning. In some classes, the children were still clicking with the workbooks far more months into the year; in others, they seemed to be getting restless and rushing through the pages. As Yogi Berra, beloved baseball philosopher, once said, "You learn a lot by looking." So we went into the classes and started looking at student independent practice time.

At this point, most teachers were bought in to systematic phonics, but the differences in how everyone was making use of *Explode the Code* were crystal clear. In the classes where children were still doing well with the workbooks, the teachers were active during student work time, evaluated student work, and went over the work with students. In the other classrooms, the books just lived in the children's desks, and the teachers tended to disengage while the students worked independently. This is probably why workbooks and worksheets got such a bad reputation even though they're efficient ways for students to gain mastery when used judiciously. Children need feedback and take things more seriously when they know their teachers are.

We didn't believe then, and still don't, that this was the teachers' fault. This was the way workbooks had come to be used, and teachers were doing what they thought the protocol was for doing workbooks. A final thought on workbooks: They are far superior to worksheets! Running off, distributing, and collecting worksheets takes far more teacher time. Forget about any but the most organized children keeping them neat and organized. The inside of classroom desks where worksheets are in circulation generally look like they were visited by localized tornadoes.

Putting This Learning into Context for Children

We've talked about scope and sequence and about direct and explicit teaching of phonics elements in a focused way. And we've discussed why that was important. What's left to discuss is putting this learning into context for children and what children should read in a systematic phonics classroom. Here's how this is discussed in the NRP Report. Read it carefully. This is a source of disagreement to this day.

> *Systematic phonics instruction typically involves explicitly teaching students a pre-specified set of letter sound relations and having students read text that provides practice using these relations to decode words. Instruction lacking an emphasis on phonics instruction does not teach letter-sound relations systematically and selects text for children according to other principles. . . .*
>
> *The latter form of instruction includes whole word programs, whole language programs, and some basal reader programs.* (NRP, 2-92)

Balanced literacy programs as currently structured have children turn to either leveled readers or trade literature after they've been taught a minilesson in phonics. In both instances, those are texts chosen "according to other principles." But this doesn't have to be this way! Nothing would be better than adopting a full-fledged systematic phonics approach, including decodable reading books so children could practice what they've been learning during guided reading. Folding those elements into the friendly structures of balanced literacy would be terrific. That has not, sadly, been the practice.

The NRP goes on to note:

> *Some systematic phonics programs are designed so that children are taught letter-sound correspondences and then provided with little books written carefully to contain the letter-sound relations that were taught.*
>
> *Some programs begin with a very limited set and expand these gradually. The intent of providing books that match children's letter-sound knowledge is to enable them to experience success in decoding words that follow the patterns they know. The stories in such books often involve pigs doing jigs and cats in hats . . . Systematic phonics programs vary in the percentage of decodable words in 1st-grade stories.* (NRP, 2-97)

And finally: "Surprisingly, very little research has attempted to determine the contribution of decodable books to the effectiveness of phonics programs" (NRP, 2-97).

Take a moment now, close the book, get a snack, and think for a moment about this. What causes all the controversy and has at least since the late 1990s?

Write your thoughts below.

Welcome back! If you landed on, "pigs and jigs" or "cats in hats," you were right. Some publishers and schools and teachers interpreted the NRP's ". . . texts that provide practice using these relations" to mean small books with most words containing phonics patterns already taught or being taught, maybe with a few with high-frequency words taught as wholes. Many teachers, other educators, and parents did not want their children's first exposure to books and reading to be simple, silly texts about, pigs and jigs or cats in hats, Dr. Seuss aside.

This is completely understandable and makes sense.

Or does it?

What we said to ourselves at the Family Academy was we were reading out loud all the time (and we did, through fifth grade, 45 minutes throughout the day), classic picture books, beautiful books that were windows into other worlds or that held mirrors up to our children's cultures and worlds. We read chapter books, even to our kindergarteners: *Charlotte's Web, The Stories Julian Tells*, books we knew our students would delight in encountering again in a couple of years with themselves in the readers' roles. How could this not produce a love of reading? We knew it did. Also, every day, the first part of the morning was free reading where students spent 15 minutes choosing any book they wanted to read. Our children loved books and loved reading as much as any students we've ever known anywhere and, certainly, more than any struggling readers we knew. Worth noting: We often saw children who were working harder to master phonics patterns would choose the decodables to read during free reading. We surmised those were the books they felt successful with, so they were drawn back to them.

We adults also tend to forget that, for children learning to read, recognizing words in print is very much its own reward. It is super exciting to see those little shapes on a page resolve into known patterns and words and to be able to read those words and sentences for yourself. Although we know very well that reading doesn't happen by magic, being with children who are new readers and are newly discovering their abilities and watching those faces light up certainly feels magical.

So we have no evidence, in our own experience or in the research base, that systematic phonics and reading a highly decodable little book will kill a love of reading. And we know at least some systematic phonics programs include some pretty silly decodable readers complete with pigs doing jigs. In a really good news story, the programs we present in the appendix all have marvelous decodable texts or move students out into trade literature through rigorous study so quickly that the quality of the decodables in the early going doesn't matter. They are that temporary.

Here's more of what we know from the NRP: "Systematic phonics programs vary in the percentage of decodable words in 1st-grade stories" and ". . . very little research has attempted to determine the contribution of decodable books to the effectiveness of phonics programs" (NRP, 2-97). Clearly, the NRP left this issue hanging; we don't even know how decodable the decodables were in the studies the NRP looked at. They're also clear that *they* don't know to what extent decodable texts contributed to the effectiveness of the systematic phonics programs.

There have been some other studies since the NRP but not many. This is a great PhD dissertation waiting to happen if anyone's looking for a topic!

Here's a summary of what we know when we combine the research from the NRP with research since:

- There is no evidence that children should read *only* decodable texts, we don't know of anyone advocating for that, nor did the NRP advocate for that.
- There is no research showing us how decodable a decodable needs to be. The benefits of decodable texts have been seen with texts at a wide variety of decodablity levels (Cheatham & Allor, 2012).
- Children early on need to learn many high-frequency words as wholes, whether phonetically regular (it, had, but, him) or irregular (the, to, of, there). They need these words to be able to read sentences and to expand their universe of known words. For words containing yet-to-be-taught sound and spelling patterns or highly irregular spellings, teachers should connect learning of new high-frequency words to known sound and spelling patterns as much as possible (e.g., in the word *to* the 't' sounds like we would expect, but in this word 'o' sounds like/o͞o).
- Although we know of no research directly addressing this, it makes sense children need an assortment of texts in kindergarten to second grade beyond strictly decodable reading books. Students need to see texts with a variety of word types, syntactic features, and different genres. They need to work with books written for a variety of purposes. Many reading researchers feel passionately about this although they acknowledge the evidence is lacking for what the right "reading diet" is exactly. Both Freddy Hiebert and Tim Shanahan have been instrumental in teaching us the importance of this idea.[2]
- Adams has thought about this a lot. The best use of decodable texts is as early as possible in kindergarten and first grade so children get those patterns into their long-term working memory as soon as possible. It's terribly important that children learn right away that words can be known and read. They need to start right away to apply the phonics patterns they've learned. That way, they'll learn what Marilyn Adams calls, "the inclination to do so." This is in opposition to eyes leaping immediately off the word and onto the picture cues or

[2] For excellent discussions on this topic, go to Hiebert's Text Project.org and type "beginning reading" into the search bar, or to ShanahanonLiteracy.org, go to his Blog and search for "decodable text."

guessing or looking beseechingly into the teacher's eyes in an appeal for assistance.

- Regardless of students' "reading diet," learning phonics patterns is essential to accurate and automatic decoding.

You may be remembering at this point that we used only decodables at the Family Academy and got great results. We did, but we moved our children into trade literature as soon as they had finished working through the sequence from *Recipe for Reading* and their decoding was automatic and approaching fluent. That sometimes happened as early as late winter of first grade or as late as the middle of third grade. Also, you'll see in the next chapter that our work with fluency beginning right away in second grade was with varied text types and offset the decodable text-heavy approach we used in kindergarten and first grade. We do wonder now, knowing more, whether having had our students read a greater variety of text types in kindergarten and first grade, along with all our reading aloud, would have made our students' comprehension better than it was when they went to third grade.

Systematic phonics programs often recommend grouping students for foundational skills, and these students will move quickly and will soon be reading trade literature. At the Family Academy, some children moved much faster through the scope and sequence than others. Those children were reading trade literature by the middle of first grade (books like *Frog and Toad*). By the end of the first quarter of second grade, nearly all students were reading trade literature, books like *The Stories Julian Tells* and *Amelia Bedelia*. Because of our fluency program (the subject of the next chapter), nearly all basic foundational skills were pretty much in place by the end of second grade most years. Some students move faster than others, some a lot faster. The inverse is true as well. What's important is that children's developmental reading needs get taken care of all across the spectrum.

So, we now know that a mix of texts including decodables is the way to go. But this still leaves a lot of questions. What should the mix be? What other types of books go into this mix? Is instruction the same for each text type?

Before you go on, spend some time responding to these questions and raising some wonderings of your own.

What's the role of practice and why is it so important?

What reflections do you have at this point?

What's the biggest take away you have at this point?

First, let's turn to how we use this mix of texts to support all students becoming readers. We're going to focus first on the decodable reading books, decodables for short.

Similar to free phonics activities, a quick search of "free decodables" will call up many. Most of the ones we scanned include information regardingwhat phonics patterns each book includes. Also, Learning A-Z, available with a modest annual subscription, has decodables and provides a scope and sequence for their use. EL Education and CKLA both have complete, self-contained scope and sequences as well as decodable readers, lessons, assessments, and everything you could need for what it costs to print and organize the materials. So you can go solo if you must for the low cost. It's better if your school or district is in a position to and on board with purchasing an excellent core ELA program that gets foundational skills right. Or you can select a high-quality foundational skills program that can stand alone, containing all the research-based ingredients you've been reading about if you feel confident all the other pieces of your ELA curriculum are effective. We describe some of these, too, at the end of the chapter. Back to the decodables and decodable text.

There are two prerequisites for a word to be decodable for a child. It has to have all regular phonics patterns, and students need to know those patterns. This does *not* mean students learned the *words* themselves in direct instruction before reading the book. It *does* mean they have learned the phonics pattern contained in those words before reading the book. For example, they may have studied all the consonant sounds and the /ŏ / patterns. They may have read as examples in instruction or practice words such as *not*, *hot*, and *pot* but not used or even seen *fog*. But fog is a regular / ŏ/ word, so they would be expected to decode it successfully.

This raises the question of whether everything in the word needs to be completely known. For example, if children have learned the "br" consonant blend and /ĭ/, can they read *brick* without having learned the sound "ck" signifies at the end of the word? Yes, for sure. They know enough about /c/ and /k/ to make an educated guess. If the /br/ blend and /ĭ/ pattern have been well planted in long-term memory, the chances of recognizing *brick* and starting the process of planting the sound "ck" makes into long-term memory is much greater. In a systematic phonics program that uses decodable texts early in students' reading instruction, it is more likely that students will be attentive to the letters and the sounds they represent. A faster learner would need fewer exposures to /ck/ and will probably infer more patterns than a student who needs more exposures before knowledge is firmed up. That same quicker student will need accordingly fewer repetitions. Other students will need more until they too get a good stock of patterns firmly installed in their long-term working memory. It is really important to remember (here and when you're working with your young charges) that all of this "fast" and "slow" business has *nothing to do with intelligence.* It is a completely different part of the brain that recognizes a symbol, associates it with a sound, and blends all the symbols that are close together into a recognizable word.

The example with *brick* is instructive because it shows why a decodable reader doesn't have to be 100% decodable. As noted, we don't know exactly what percentage of decodability is needed for a decodable to support student reading. Studies confirming the value of using decodable readers ranged widely in what percentage of the words were decodable.

What is clear from the research is that decodables are best used in kindergarten and first grade but do not have to be the only texts students read. Here's the problem. We've generally found many schools and teachers, even those that use decodables, don't get nearly as much out of them as they can for their children and in some combination are failing to do one or more of these things:

- devote enough time to them (differentially), with students who need more time getting more access;
- include any comprehension questions so children learn they're supposed to think about what they've read and expect it to make some sense;
- provide support for any vocabulary students might not know; and/or
- mine the decodable reader for all it has to offer.

Here's a multiday protocol for using decodables that demonstrates just how much good learning you can get from them. It works equally well for small-group instruction or whole class:

We want to give you a sense of the range of games you can do with your children. We've departed from our /ĕ/ lesson by now to give you examples. Some of these may take some explaining and trial runs before you and your students get the hang of them, but stick with them. They make everything ever so much more fun, and learning is ever so much better if it can also be fun! These protocols and the ones that follow for less-decodable texts call for a lot

Read No.	Format	Notes	Instructional Purpose
First	Whole class or group *OR* students read independently if you want a baseline sense of what might trouble your students right away	Teacher reads while students follow along, finger pointing at each word as teacher reads until they get in the habit of following. Teacher should read with expression. Teacher explains in student-friendly terms the meanings of any words students might not know (first see if any students can determine from context). Students whisper read each word and spell it.	Students hear a fluent read. Students hear and see the new phonics pattern. This is the first step in beginning to plant the pattern into long-term memory. *Any* opportunity to grow vocabulary should be taken if you think children might not know the meaning of the words they're encountering. Also, it is harder for children to decode and read with fluency when there are too many words they don't know the meaning of. Never lose a chance to make reading meaning filled! Words are best learned and stored in a student's long-term memory when spelling, meaning, and pronunciation are integrated as much as possible. Each reinforces the other. Knowing how to spell a word helps in recalling its meaning; knowing meaning helps in remembering its spelling. They are mutually reinforcing cognitive tasks.

Continued on next page

Read No.	Format	Notes	Instructional Purpose
Second	Choral[3]	Teacher leads choral reading Note: • which students are struggling • which words present hesitations Follow with basic comprehension questions.	Students can hear *and experience* a fluent read. Teacher can note where she hears hesitation by the group around certain words. If these are words containing patterns already taught, this signals these patterns may need some more work. The newest pattern *should* produce more hesitation; if it doesn't, it could be a signal the pattern is not that difficult for this group. Students should be picked randomly to answer these questions to see who isn't comprehending. This sends the message that even in skills work comprehension is always the goal. Basic comprehension should go before the more text-based questions (see the following). Basic questions are questions such as who is in the story, what is happening, where, etc. This reinforces that reading is for making meaning and helps all students' understanding.

Continued on next page

[3] This will be covered more in-depth in the next chapter (Reading Fluency), but a choral reading means everyone in the group reads the story together like they're a musical chorus. The teacher should read quietly enough to hear and monitor the children's reading for accuracy.

Read No.	Format	Notes	Instructional Purpose
Third	Students read out loud to themselves or buddy read	Allow time for independent reading. Teacher monitors for word challenges.	Allows students to all work independently. Teacher can monitor individual needs. If necessary, teacher can take the students who need significant support to accurately decode and read with them.
Fourth	Echo or choral[4]	If more support is needed, use echo reading; if less, use choral. Or start with echo reading and shift to choral. If you are comfortable with how well students are doing, including reading with some fluency, you can skip to the next step here. Follow this with time for more complex comprehension questions. Samples can be found in the following. Cold call for questions, listen to students discuss what they think, or let them write their answers. Vary the types of responses you ask for to give children varied experiences.	This provides more practice with the new phonics pattern as well as all the others that are in the text. Although not as good as buddy reading, this gives you another opportunity to listen for students who are still struggling. At this point, if a student is still struggling, you know she needs more support, which can come in the next step This is a good time to focus on reading with expression. Gives time to assess any and all comprehension needs; it is important that all students are fully comprehending the text at this point and are aware that comprehension is the purpose for reading.

Continued on next page

[4] This, too, will be covered more in the next chapter, but an echo read is like a call and response. The teacher reads a chunk of the text while students follow silently, then all students in the group echo what the teacher just read. This pattern is continued through the text.

Read No.	Format	Notes	Instructional Purpose
		When students give their answers, be sure to reread aloud the portion of the text that proves their answer.	Returning to text and reading aloud gives all students another swing through the text, helping reinforce learning phonics patterns. It also starts to establish the habit of using text evidence when answering questions.
Fifth	Buddy/paired reading	One student reads, one follows along, and then they switch roles. Children can switch every page or two, depending on the length of the pages and how they're doing.	At this point, you should know who isn't reading with accuracy and at a decent rate. You can decide to "buddy up" with anyone that still needs more support, or if you have concerns about several students, you can make a group of children who need more attention during this time. This gives you a chance to get a better picture and provide even more support.
Later	Foundational skills games and activities	Text-based games and tasks that reinforce phonics patterns and support student fun with language.	See the following samples.

<table>
<tr><td colspan="2">Comprehension Questions (Samples): These are the comprehension questions for the third read. Allow time for students to return to the text to answer questions.</td></tr>
<tr><th>Sample Questions</th><th>Instructional Purpose</th></tr>
<tr><td>• How many things did they (characters) get scared of or worried about all together?
• What insect did the boys worry about?
• Reread page 7. When it says, "Dad helped them," who is "them"?
• Reread page 8. Why does James say, "It is like home"?
• How many questions do the boys ask in this story?
• Dad helps James and Sam in two different ways. What are those two ways?</td><td>Even with a relatively simple book, this group of questions focuses on comprehending a number of events in the text, tracing a pronoun reference, and making an inference.
The following are possible text-dependent generic questions to include. These can be asked of any text.
What is the title of this [story/text/passage]? Why do you think it is called that?
Who are the characters in this story? (fiction)
What problem do they have? How do they solve it? (fiction)
What is this text mostly about? (informational)
What new ideas/facts did you learn? (informational)</td></tr>
</table>

of repetition. We should talk about this because it probably seems like a lot of repetition to you. And it is! First, you can and should adjust this based on your sense of children's needs. *Every* one of them. As we've noted quite a few times, some children won't need this much repetition. That being said, repetition is recommended by *every* cognitive scientist who writes about and studies how

<table>
<tr><th colspan="3">Sample Phonics Games and Activities</th></tr>
<tr><th>Page</th><th>Question/Tasks</th><th>Instructional Purpose</th></tr>
<tr><td>1</td><td>• What letter is making the vowel sound in every word? [multiple answers]
• If you put an 'e' at the end of Sam, what word do you get? Pronounce it. [same]
• If you take away the first letter of the fourth word, what letter can you replace it with that gives you something you can eat? [make/cake]
• What letter can you add to the third word to make it rhyme with the sixth word? [random]</td><td>• Reinforcing vowel sounds and the concept of vowel sounds
• "Magic e"
• Phoneme substitution
• Rhyming</td></tr>
</table>

Sample Phonics Games and Activities		
Page	**Question/Tasks**	**Instructional Purpose**
2	• Which word is the same spelled forward and backward? [wow] • If you take away the first letter of the second word and replace it with the first letter of the first word, you get something sweet, what is it? Pronounce it. [his money/honey] • Does the letter 'a' make the same sound in *Sam* as it does in *James*? [no]	• Initial and ending sound • Phoneme substitution • Comparing sounds (consonant-vowel-consonant [CVC] vs. CVCe)
3	• There are two ways the /e/ sound is spelled on this page, what are they? [varies] • What word ends with a /z/ sound? [his] • What letters are making the /a/ sound in the first word on this page? [multiple /ā/ words]	• Vowel sound spelling • Final consonant sounds • Vowel sound spelling
4	• How many words can you make by taking away the first letter of the fifth word on this page and adding another different letter? The added letter does not have to be from this page. [random] • What are the words you see twice on this page? What vowel sound do they have? [random]	• Phoneme manipulation • Attention to words, vowel sound
5	• What word on this page rhymes with a number? [fix/six] • What word on this page, if you take away the first letter, gives you something you can do with your tongue? [slick/lick]	• Rhyming • Phoneme deletion
6	• Take away the last letter of this word and add an 'l' at the end, and it gives you something you take when you are sick. What is the word? [pile/pill] • Change the first letter of this word from an 'f' to a 't,' and it makes something that is on a car. What is the word? [fire/tire]	• Phoneme manipulation • Initial sounds

children learn to read. It is automaticity that necessitates the repetition. Whenever we are in a school and asked to help with older students who are reading poorly, we ask to have some of them read to one of us privately. Many times, students will recognize the words and pronounce them correctly, even words they don't know the meaning of. But it is always *far* too slow. Somewhere along the line, these students learned many, if not all, of the phonics patterns that can spell the 44 sounds of the English language. But they never got the chance to have the repetition they needed to decode with automaticity. Recall proficient readers recognize words in about a quarter of a second. These students were taking more like 10 seconds, far too long to read with fluency or integrate the meaning of the word into the sentence. This is so because by the time they finished decoding the word they would have forgotten much of what came before. If too much mental activity goes into decoding, little is left for comprehension.

We've already told you our goal! We want *every single* child decoding automatically by the end of first grade and fluently by the end of second grade. That's based on our knowledge and a ton of research that children who aren't able to do these things tend to not read well. Poor readers suffer lifelong consequences. The stakes are high. So be sure your students are all set before you move them on.

One day David was lounging around with our oldest grandson watching *Paw Patrol*, which he said was his favorite show. At every key juncture, he told me *exactly* what was going to happen next. I knew he was a smart kid, but this was ridiculous. Later, I was exclaiming about this ability with his mother, but she set me straight. She told me the show was so beloved, recording and replaying the same episode numerous times was the norm, and that was what I had experienced. An inexpensive hit formula! The fact is children love repetition, they love rituals and routines, they love to know what is going to happen, and they love being good at something in general.[5] These protocols bring all of that together.

Another note: this time on the alphabetic principle and language. The third column ("Instructional Purpose") of the sample games and phonics activities just scratches the surface of what these games teach. Far more than each of the listed elements is the alphabetic principle, the idea that letters are references for sounds, and the beginnings of an understanding of the power of language. Understanding that if you change one letter you change the entire meaning of a word is a stepping stone to understanding the power of words. It is also great fun. There are very few people if any who love words, love language, and are not proficient readers.

Let's wrap up with what is the most important reason to use decodables in a systematic phonics program. It does no good to teach phonics if students

---

[5] Repetition and ritual in children's television is a demonstrated winning formula. If you're familiar with *Blues Clues* or interested in this topic for multimedia programming, here is a quick read: https://en.wikipedia.org/wiki/Blue%27s_Clues.

don't use it in learning to read. Kids aren't stupid; they're short. If, in the only books they're asked to read, children can't use learned phonics patterns or can only use them a few times, they'll stop using them. This is why decodables are essential, especially for the children we need to help the most in school (those who don't have much experience with books when they step into kindergarten). To teach phonics and then give children a diet of books in which they can't use what they've learned to make sense of reading would make the entire literacy world even less meaningful. For too many children, this is what happens even if they do have a systematic phonics program if the only texts they read are leveled readers where phonics knowledge helps only a little or not at all.

But we said students need to read different text types. So what about those texts that are not decodables? To some extent, this depends on the characteristics of the other books that are in use. In most cases, these are the leveled readers many of us are familiar with. Other possibilities are content-based books about topics students are studying, high-frequency readers that emphasize the most frequent words in English, and of course, trade literature.

The best way to approach these other books is also by using a protocol so you can consciously replicate or contrast the experiences with how you're using decodables. Keep in mind that you should approach these books differently from how you may have before you started teaching phonics systematically. There is more than one type of these early reader books. Some, especially for early kindergarten, may be much like decodables. You also may be using a core ELA program and not have time to follow all of this procedure. That's fine as long as you feel good about the quality of learning those materials are providing your students.

Non-Decodables Protocol for Reinforcing Learning

We know many teachers have their own system for asking questions and ascertaining children's learning from their own existing program or resources. What we are modeling in this protocol is how many (fun) ways there are to hold children accountable for words with patterns they already know and how to pay close attention to new words to see if they can grow their phonics knowledge. All along, it's important they develop the habit of using decoding—focusing on the word itself—as their first tool for figuring out what unknown words might be.

Here are some generic text-dependent questions that could be asked with any text, decodable or not. Although the best questions are specific to the book you're reading, these are good stand-ins that will work for most early books. Of course, you can also use your grade-level reading standards as a guide, as well.

Read No.	Format	Notes	Instructional Implications	Differences and Similarities from Decodables
First	Read aloud while students follow along.	Be sure children finger point to each word as you read. Keep this up until they're accustomed to following along reliably. You should read with expression but at a somewhat slower rate than normal. A good way to think of it is at about three-quarter speed.	Students will hear a fluent reading modeled while they see and hear words with phonics patterns they know and ones they don't. Weaker readers will have a better chance of developing an initial understanding of the text, a potential issue even with a text designed to be at their level.	As with the decodables, seeing and hearing the word while focusing on the word through finger pointing will help students learn phonic patterns. With more phonics patterns present that students haven't learned, the slower pace will help students focus better on these words.
Second	Read aloud (with student's finger pointing). This time, stop to explain any words or references students might not know, asking first if they can figure these out from context.	After the meaning of the word is explained, ask students to look at the word again and whisper read the word, spell it, and say its meaning to themselves.	Much research shows that word learning is best done when meaning, spelling, and pronunciation are locked together as much as possible and students read and spell the word aloud.	The teacher read-aloud instead of the choral read with the decodables supports comprehension. This time, the students' following along is primarily for vocabulary growth as well as holding students accountable for following along for learning how to pronounce words and patterns new to them.

Read No.	Format	Notes	Instructional Implications	Differences and Similarities from Decodables
	For informational text, ask students what they think this reading is mostly about. For literary narratives, ask what happened in the story.	When this is completed, repeat the same procedure with a partner. Chose children randomly for these questions so everyone knows they may have to answer questions and has an obligation to think.	Support for vocabulary will help comprehension and support English-language learners and other students with smaller vocabularies. Students should get the gist of the text or a sense of its main idea before addressing more specific or complex questions.	Some of these books may be more complex than decodables, and comprehension at this level will make further reads more fruitful and support more inferential and specific questions in later reads. True of the decodables as well but less support for decoding here generally makes these readings less accessible.
Third	Children buddy-read, taking turns by paragraph or page. When one child is reading, the other is following along with a finger. Pairs who finish early should pick their favorite part and continue the same system.	Consider taking the weakest readers and "buddying" with them. If not, listen in to see how these readers are doing. Some children always finish before others. Be sure the pairs know this before they start so they don't rush through.	This provides another swing through the text to further support mastery of phonics patterns and reading fluency. Of course, this helps with comprehension as well.	As these texts could be more complex than decodables (and will by definition have phonics patterns students don't know), the buddy read provides more support before students read on their own.

Continued on next page

Read No.	Format	Notes	Instructional Implications	Differences and Similarities from Decodables
Fourth	Format for discussion (or written response) is up to you. You could mix it up by taking the weakest readers with you, the strongest readers work individually, and others work in pairs. Suggested basic questions follow this chart.	By now, many students will have a good sense of the text and will be ready for more inferential questions. Responses can be in writing, in discussion, or a mix. Be sure to go over the children's answers and provide feedback. Be sure to ask them to return to the text for evidence and reread the portion of the text that provides it.	Starting comprehension questions after vocabulary work and multiple reads helps support all children's comprehension and develops confidence. Bringing students back to the text means more chances to learn phonics patterns through reading and hearing the words yet again. It also reinforces an emphasis on text evidence.	The fourth and fifth reads of the text are the independent reads. They address decoding and fluency and especially finding out who is still struggling in these areas.
Fifth	Point out words with phonics patterns new to students.	Best done in buddy pairs. Ask each pair to find as many words as they can with a phonics pattern they have *not learned* and then try to determine what letters or combinations of letters make each sound in the word.	This reinforces the alphabetic principle, introduces students to new phonics patterns, and grows a greater understanding of the different types of texts students will be reading in these years.	

- What is the title of this [story/text/passage]?
- Who are the characters in this story? (fiction)
- What problem do they have? How do they solve it? (fiction)
- What is this text mostly about? (informational)
- What did you learn from reading this text? (any text, but essential for informational)
- What did this text make you wonder about? (any text)

As we noted earlier, The Text Project,[6] a labor of love and knowledge by the generous reading researcher Elfrieda (Freddy) Hiebert, has a series called "Beginning Reads," which is in some ways, a genre all its own. These books are designed beautifully both to follow research on what young readers need and to be easy to print, fold, and use. The books repeat words as often as possible, minimizing how often a word only appears once, and deliberately use words children are likely to see in other books they will be reading in these early years. They come complete with word cards for vocabulary instruction, "Reader's Theater," and a variety of supports and suggestions for use. All are free, and the books read-aloud can be found on iTunes as well as on The Text Project website. We see these as far more supportive and effective for children than traditional leveled readers.

A Quick Aside on Comprehension Instruction

We feel very strongly the best comprehension instruction in kindergarten through second grade is through read-aloud. That's because there's no ceiling on complexity or richness the way there has to be in books for new readers. Children access meaning through their ears and can think deeply about complex ideas and characters if the hard cognitive work of decoding is lifted out of the equation. Books for read-aloud can easily be two or three years above the *class* grade level. So read-aloud books will inevitably be more complex, be richer, and contain far more vocabulary and more interesting sentence patterns. So they'll invite deeper questions than almost anything most children in that grade can read to themselves. Read aloud also "levels the playing field" for your students, especially if you make it interactive, actively teach vocabulary, and have lots of text-based discussions. Everybody has access to the language and riches of the book regardless of how well they are currently progressing in learning to read.

Please don't make the mistake of thinking read aloud isn't teaching reading; this is as wrong-headed as it gets. In addition to the vocabulary and

[6] The Text Project: www.textproject.org.

knowledge gained during it, listening comprehension correlates strongly with reading comprehension once decoding is solidly in place. But this book is about foundational skills, although we're having so much fun writing it, we'd be happy to write another one about comprehension in pre-K to second grade. If you're having fun or finding value too, ask for more!

So where are we now? We've talked about the need for a scope and sequence, discussed the importance of direct and explicit instruction, established how crucial focused practice out of context is, and examined how to approach the books children read (in context work).

Take a break. Before turning to the next page and final section, guess what comes next.

If you guessed assessment you're right on target.

Assessing Student Learning

Here's how to do it if you want to be sure your students are mastering each phonics pattern you teach them: You dictate to them and have them spell words that contain the pattern. If a child can spell a word correctly in roughly 30 seconds, it is likely she can easily read it with grade-appropriate automaticity. So we recommend a very straightforward assessment. Each week, dictate five or six words with that week's phonics pattern. For example, this week you worked with the /oy/ diphthong spelled with 'oi.' So you could dictate *boil*, *void*, *toil*, *oil*, and *poison*. For each word, be sure to say the word slowly, put it in a sentence, and repeat it again slowly. Make sure your students know what the words mean, too (even during assessment you can teach new vocabulary if you didn't encounter and teach the meaning of these words earlier!). Wait no more than 30 seconds before going on to the next word. Following this, cycle in a couple of words containing sound and spelling patterns from past lessons to make sure previous patterns have stuck. Use the same procedure.

There's a factor here that can confound results. Children may have seen many of these words during the week's work and memorized the spelling. This is why nonsense words were invented! For the last part of your assessment, make up two nonsense words (and then follow the same procedure). Nonsense words, sometimes called pseudo words, have regular spelling patterns but are not words, so they can act as pure assessment tools in phonics. For example, in this case, you could use *soid* and *loik* as two nonsense words. The nonsense words don't need sentences unless you and your students are in a silly mood and want to play with the made-up words.

One thing to remember: Sooner or later, your systematic scope and sequence is going to be introducing multiple ways to represent the same sound. After all, there are about 150 spellings in written English but just 44 phonemes, so lots of sounds can be made in several ways. Think of long vowels in particular. The /Ā/ sound can be made in these seven ways: *slay, sleigh, sale, rain, apron, hey, great.* Or think of /oi/. It can also be spelled as 'oy,' and it's very likely you already taught it that way; think of *boy, toy,* and *joy.* But there's also *boil* and *soil.* Some programs speed up after a slower start and introduce multiple spellings for one sound within the same week. There are two takeaways for this. One is simple. On your nonsense words, accept any spelling of the phonic sound the children have been exposed to. With real words, children will solidify their standard spelling when they've seen and worked with words a lot. They'll know that *boy* and *toy* are spelled with a 'y' but *boil* has the 'oi' spelling. For now, you can celebrate either spelling because it shows the awareness of the phonics pattern is solid.

Assessing is about knowing who knows what. Just as important as knowing is what you do with the results of assessments. We have found over and over again that the schools that succeed with reading are those that had a clear, concrete, manageable protocol for what to do with students who did poorly on the weekly assessment. Most schools either supported these students in a designated weekly tier two intervention or used small groups or center time to go back and quickly fill in gaps in understanding. What drove the success was everyone knew what to do, had time to do it, and had access to the right materials for reteaching. A great teacher can do this on her own, and too many of you have had to, but this truly should be an "it takes a village" effort to organize around every child's early literacy success. The CKLA Skill program, which we've mentioned before, has an amazing resource called the *Assessment and Remediation Guide.* It's free to download on the CoreKnowledge.org website and on EngageNY.[7] This is the size of an old New York City telephone book! It has weekly assessments and then multiple materials for absolutely every phonics pattern. It's ideal for this purpose and is a model of how assessment and reteaching based on the results should work.

When should you offer more experiences with an unlearned phonics pattern? As a rule of thumb, ideally, you would offer students more explicit support and learning if, after a week's worth of focused work on a pattern, some children are still not getting it.

[7] Core Knowledge *Assessment and Remediation Guide* can be found at the Foundation's website for free download: https://www.coreknowledge.org/wp-content/uploads/2017/01/CKLA_G3_ARG_web.pdf or on EngageNY (broken out by grade, this link will take you to second grade): https://www.engageny.org/resource/grade-2-ela-skills-strand-assessment-and-remediation-guides.

Wrap-Up

We're almost there! You've read about the importance of a scope and sequence for phonics. You know that phonics patterns, once planted in long-term memory, enable children (and us) to rapidly and effortlessly recognize the words on a page—even if some of those words aren't in our vocabulary, we'll know how to pronounce them. You know the importance of both out-of-context practice and practice in context (with books), and we've just looked at a simple, powerful regimen for weekly assessment and the importance of acting on those results weekly. We've gone through what constitutes a systematic phonics program.

This was a long chapter! If you still want more, you can find free resources on achievethecore.org.

The "Foundational Skills Guidance Documents"[8] offer great general information. If you want a verve-filled immersion course, the 8-hour "Foundational Skills Mini Course" taught by David and our colleague, the extraordinary Carey Swanson, is also available.

Without successful and automatic decoding, students cannot read fluently. Decoding will take you a lot of the way but not all the way to successful reading. Students still need to know how to read words within and across sentences and to read smoothly at a rate and with expressiveness both appropriate to the text. This is fluency, what Tim Rasinski, the leading fluency researcher, has called "the bridge to comprehension." We believe it is that and even more, and we address it in the next chapter. A great fluency program can *to a certain extent* make up for some unfinished work in foundational skills, and we'll look at those possibilities in our final chapter.

[8] Foundational Skills Guidance Documents and access to the Mini Course: https://achievethecore.org/category/1206/ela-literacy-foundational-skills.

Sources for Deeper Learning and Teaching

Explode the Code Books A, B, C, and 1–8

Educational Publishing Service, Cambridge, MA
http://eps.schoolspecialty.com/products/literacy/phonics-word-study/explode-the-code/about-the-program

Search for "44 Phonemes" on YouTube for the best video we've seen on precise pronunciation

This is from the Rollins University Center on Language and Literacy and was retrieved January 1, 2019.

https://www.youtube.com/watch?v=wBuA589kfMg

The Text Project is a comprehensive resource site that even has free, downloadable readers. Everything is free on the site.

www.textproject.org

Works Consulted

Bus, A. G., & van IJzendoorn, M. H. (1999). Phonological awareness and early reading: A meta-analysis of experimental training studies. *Journal of Educational Psychology*, *91*, 403.

Cheatham, J. P., & Allor, J. (2012) The influence of decodability in early reading text on reading achievement: A review of the evidence. *Reading and Writing*, *25*. doi:10.1007/s11145-011-9355-2

D'angiulli, A., Siegel, L. S., & Maggi, M. (2004). Literacy instruction, SES, and word-reading achievement in English-language learners and children with English as a first language: A longitudinal study. *Learning Disabilities Research & Practice*, *19*, 202–213. doi:10.1111/j.1540-5826.2004.00106.x

Joshi, R. M., Dahlgren, M., & Boulware-Gooden, R. (2002). Teaching reading in an inner city school through a multisensory teaching approach. *Annals of Dyslexia*, *52*, 229–242.

Landi, N., Perfetti, C. A., Bolger, D. J., Dunlap, S., & Foorman, B. R. (2006). The role of discourse context in developing word form representations: A paradoxical relation between reading and learning. *Journal of Experimental Child Psychology*, *94*, 114–133. doi:10.1016/j.jecp.2005.12.004

McGaugh, J. L. (2006). Make mild moments memorable: Add a little arousal. *Trends in Cognitive Sciences*, *10*, 345–347. doi:10.1016/j.tics.2006.06.001

Mesmer, H. A. E., & Griffith, P. L. (2005). Everybody's selling it—But just what is explicit, systematic phonics instruction? *The Reading Teacher*, *59*, 366–376. doi:10.1598/RT.59.4.6

National Reading Panel (US) & National Institute of Child Health and Human Development (US). (2000). *Report of the National Reading Panel: Teaching children to read: An evidence-based assessment of the scientific research literature on reading and its implications for reading instruction: Reports of the subgroups*. Bethesda, MD: National Institute of Child Health and Human Development, National Institutes of Health.

Phillips, W. E., & Feng, J. (2012). *Methods for sight word recognition in kindergarten: Traditional flashcard method vs. multisensory approach.* Paper presented at the Annual Conference of the Georgia Educational Research Association, Savannah, GA.

Scheffel, D. L., Shaw, J. C., & Shaw, R. (2008). The efficacy of a supplementary multisensory reading program for first-grade students. *Journal of Reading Improvement*, *45*, 139–152.

Chapter Six

Reading Fluency: A Story

It was mid-March, in the doldrums of the New York City school calendar. You wouldn't know that in our second-grade classrooms. The second-graders were preparing for their Public Reading, one of our favorite rituals. They had already experienced one, so they were giddy with excitement and nerves, remembering how much praise and attention they'd gotten back in November. Everyone had their chosen poem, paragraph, or set of riddles printed out fresh, in large font, so they could be read with ease. They knew their parents and older siblings would be coming as soon as they could get there, and they knew there'd be homemade cookies and punch after everyone had read.

The second-graders had departed from their usual weekly routine with our homemade "Fluency Packet" to pick their own favorite poem of the moment, some riddles they liked, or a paragraph from a book they had recently read. Each child had worked to learn the correct pronunciation and cadence for her selection and then had rehearsed her piece daily during the 15-minute fluency time for the past week and a half. Everybody was confident about their performance. Each child was reading her selection clearly and accurately, with the expressiveness the selection warranted, and loudly enough for a full room to hear. The second-graders had achieved the high level of fluency and self-confidence required for public speaking and performance.

These Public Readings were the performance outlet of our second-grade fluency program, the focused effort to ensure all our second-graders were fluent with grade-level texts before they headed off to third grade. We had found it was straightforward and doable to achieve universal reading fluency in second grade given that nearly all our first graders came in with solid decoding and automaticity with the patterns they'd been taught. Reading fluency was enshrined at the Family Academy as a nonnegotiable accomplishment by the end of second grade, just like automaticity in decoding was for first grade and phonemic awareness proficiency was for kindergarten.

Reading fluency was enshrined at the Family Academy as a nonnegotiable accomplishment by the end of second grade, just like automaticity in decoding was for first grade and phonemic awareness proficiency was for kindergarten.

How did we do it? Compared with the many moving parts of our structured phonics program you've been reading so much about, which continued, of course, into second grade with the more complex patterns getting learned, achieving reading fluency was easy.

First, let's make sure we're all on the same page in our understanding of reading fluency and how crucial it is to later reading success.

In the box, write your own working definition of reading fluency before we offer ours.

Reading fluency is:

What Exactly Is Reading Fluency?

Reading fluency is the ability to smoothly read texts you encounter, expressively and well, whether you're reading to yourself or reading aloud. Those texts should be at the complexity level of the grade the student is currently in. This means focusing on emergent reading texts in kindergarten and first grade and moving into grade-level texts in second grade and beyond.

There are three elements of fluency:

- Accuracy
- Rate (appropriate to what you're reading)
- Expressiveness (known to reading researchers and poetry scholars as prosody)

Accuracy

Accuracy means pronouncing words the way they commonly are. Ideally, by second grade, children should be able to accurately *and swiftly* pronounce any word that is made up of phonics patterns they've learned and any sight words (high-frequency words) they know. That's why getting adequate practice with new patterns so automatic decoding is achieved as they are introduced is so crucial. Automatic decoding is a necessary prerequisite to reading fluency. Accurate reading also means noticing and reading punctuation correctly. That means children need to know how punctuation works and be able to apply that knowledge automatically whenever they see common punctuation symbols (the comma, period, exclamation point, and question mark, for starters).

- Punctuation helps notate the cadence of written language so it reads similarly to the spoken word. Punctuation exists to represent the pauses, stops, and inflections speakers naturally make as part of their communication. So reading punctuation marks and being able to chunk syntax appropriately to support meaning making both support comprehension. A lot.
- There are punctuation basics children can all know as early as kindergarten through concepts of print, and certainly, students should know cold by the time they're in second grade.
- Here are the essentials:
  - Commas signal a pause in the reading (and a chance to take a quick breath). It's helpful if students also know that commas separate parts of a sentence, too. That's enough about commas in second grade.
  - There has to be end punctuation at the end of every sentence. There are three main types children need to know how to read at this point: periods, exclamation marks, and question marks. They need to know how the voice inflects for each type.
    - When we speak in declarative sentences, marked in print by periods, our voice drops.
    - When we ask questions, our voices inflect higher at the end of the question. So that's what children should do when they read a question mark. Why, you ask? Because that's how the listener learns you're asking a question.
    - Exclamation marks signal excitement or strong feelings. Our vocal inflection gets louder to signal excitement.

We've rarely encountered a child who didn't grasp and apply these punctuation lessons quickly, especially when they'd had lots of reading-aloud exposure since kindergarten.

End punctuation does more than signal the type of sentence and how it should be read. It also signals "quick break time!" and gives the reader a chance to take a full breath. Children would have learned at various points from their print awareness, read-aloud, and phonological awareness work that every sentence holds an idea. Reminding your students they can think about what the sentence they just read means for a second or two (while they're taking that breath) is a huge assist to comprehension. With poetry, for example, a terrific genre for fluency work, reading to the punctuation to understand poems is key to students' learning to appreciate and value poetry. Although there is a lot more to punctuation than this, knowing at least this will help readers of any age improve their fluency through strengthening their automatic decoding of words *and* punctuation.

Rate

Rate refers to the speed of oral reading. We're always careful to say "rate appropriate to the text being read" whenever we talk about rate. That's because there's a Goldilocks effect with reading rate. You need to read quickly enough to get a flow, so the words in a sentence hang together as a unit and the sentences unfold as you read one after the other coherently. That way, you can make sense of what the author is communicating. If you read too slowly, decoding word by word, your short-term working memory can't hold onto the earlier words. By the time you get to the end of the sentence, comprehension is long gone. But if you read too quickly, you'll only get the gist of what you read, the barest sense. You'll lose any subtlety of meaning and likely won't catch much of what the author is transmitting, let alone any of the jewels that got planted in the text along the way. If what you're reading is dense or on a topic unfamiliar to you, you need to read it more slowly than, say, a riveting novel you're reading for pleasure.

So, too, with children. They need to read within that just-right range, and they need to be told directly that different kinds of texts warrant different rates.

But how do we know what that just-right range is? There are norms established for oral reading fluency (ORF). The best known and freely available are the Hasbrouck and Tindal norms, which were updated in 2017.[1] The chart provides fall, winter, and spring percentile rates for children from grades one through six. The article linked in the footnote on this page offers important cautions from Hasbrouck about not rushing children toward the higher percentile levels. In other words, with reading rate, being average is just fine. After all, rate is only one part of reading fluency, and reading fluency is only a part of reading comprehension. Understanding what you read is the goal, whether we're children or adults, not racing to get through. You may know adult readers who read at very different rates than you do. That's true of the two of us. David barely breaks the eighth-grade mean on the norms chart, and Meredith reads quickly—too quickly? Guess which of the two of us retains *everything* he reads and who needs to force herself to slow down and read with focus and attention?

Read this next sentence as fast as you possibly can to get the idea:

> *Here's-who-should-be-striving-to-go-off-the-charts-on-those-oral-reading-fluency-norms:-children-who-want-to-grow-up-to-be-auctioneers-or-the-people-in-ads-who-oh-so-quickly-rattle-off-all-the-scary-side-effects-of-a-medication,-or-what-the-terms-are-for-canceling-a-car-lease-before-time-is-up.*

[1] For information about their updated norms, read "Fluency Norms Chart (2017 Update)" by Jan Hasbrouck and Gerald Tindal. http://www.readingrockets.org/article/fluency-norms-chart-2017-update

Those strivers will find their way to their desired future selves just fine. For all the rest of us, the goal is to read at that just-right rate that matches the demands of what we're reading. That's quicker when we're doing light reading or we only want to skim for the gist, slower if the material is dense or unfamiliar and we really want to learn from what we're reading.

For more definitive guidance, in her article introducing the new norms (noted in the following), Hasbrouck suggests we should plan extra fluency practice for those "[s]tudents scoring 10 or more words below the 50th percentile using the average score of two unpracticed readings from grade-level materials." We'll talk more about how to assess fluency and how often later in the chapter, but for now, what it means is you don't have to worry about children who are at say, the 45th percentile on up, depending on what the words correct per minute (wcpm) norms are for that child at that point in the year. This chapter draws on all of the work you've done in kindergarten and first grade to secure students' ability to decode. We'll look closely at how that plays out with the second-grade norms across the school year.

Second-graders 50th percentile	Fall: 50 wcpm	Winter: 84 wcpm	Spring: 100 wcpm

In the fall, a child who was reading fewer than 40 wcpm would worry us and need extra attention. In the fall of second grade, this is likely a child who doesn't yet have solid decoding skills, so she can't make the shift to automatic decoding of known patterns. We would want to pounce on addressing this child's needs on both the phonics and oral fluency practice fronts. In the winter, we would worry about any children reading fewer than 74 wcpm with second-grade–level texts and would want to offer more chances to practice fluency to make gains. If they are reading far more slowly than that, we should still be intervening with more direct phonics instruction, focusing on getting these children able to decode more automatically (improving their automaticity). We would also keep providing more pinpointed fluency practice. By the spring, we would want to work with any child reading fewer than 90 wcpm so they finish the year strong. Here too, the work would be in repairing any missing decoding skills, working to improve automaticity of word recall, and then doubling down on fluency work in a coached setting.

One important aspect of fluency to understand is that there's a three-way relationship between fluency and decoding and how complex the text is. Two factors make a text more complex (primarily): It has less common vocabulary, and it has more sentences with complicated syntax. So whenever readers move into reading more complex text than they're used to, they'll backslide a bit on their fluency because they're working harder at decoding less familiar phonics patterns and probably longer words. So their automaticity will need time to catch up with the new challenges. Our fluency packets, for example, were not controlled at all for familiar phonics patterns or ease of syntax. When children chose their own passages for the Public Reading performance, we didn't try to get them to read easier stuff. So that three-way relationship is good news. It means, with enough fluency practice with varied enough text, young readers will get comfortable fluently reading a wide variety of text types that range widely in complexity. This also means that fluency work needs to continue beyond second grade. Nearly all state standards include fluency and multisyllabic word study at least through fifth grade, and some continue with fluency through eighth grade. Fluency is just that important. But more on that in the final chapter.

Connected to this discussion, it's worth noting what you probably already did: that second-graders are expected to improve their reading rate 100% during the course of the year, as are first-graders (from 29 wcpm to 60 by the spring). Wow! That seems aggressive. In no other grades are such rapid increases in rate expected or advised (remember the goal is a nation of readers, not auctioneers!).

But it makes total sense that rapid growth in rate and accuracy (words *correct* per minute) is expected in these two grades. They are learning all the phonics patterns the English language holds. That means their repertoire of words they can look at and read is growing weekly. They need to get comfortable and automatic reading all those patterns. So automaticity of decoding and fluency are the two places where instructional time and children's practice efforts and energy should be focused during first and second grades. That focused work and attention will bring these increases in rate. Because these two precursors are necessary preconditions for children to be successful readers, they are worth all the time and focus. Nothing else is more important in these two years of school. Children need their brains free to think about what they're reading so they can learn stuff they want to. They can't do that if they're effortfully working out what each word is. In short, rate matters once students have moved beyond an early focus on decoding and building toward automaticity.

Expressiveness (Prosody)

Just as the name implies, prosody is reading aloud with expression suited to what you're reading. Prosody makes it pleasurable to hear someone reading aloud and helps convey meaning to listeners. Those aspects of prosody are certainly important. There is an important flip side of prosody's benefits for the reader herself and for the alert teacher who is monitoring reading progress. Prosodic reading signals that the reader understands what she's reading and is tracking and making sense of the syntax and context clues. That is crucial information for teachers to know and use. Children who are not comfortable, fluent readers tend to labor, reading in a wooden, flat voice. They are hard to listen to and, generally, hate to read aloud. That makes total sense but sets in motion a terrible cycle we'll address in the next chapter regarding older students with reading problems. But we're here with kindergarteners and first- and second-graders, and we're going to keep them on track!

There are several parts to prosody. Teachers, as educated adults, tend to do these things naturally and unselfconsciously, having mastered prosodic reading years before. But it's useful to itemize these elements and be aware of them. That way, we can model prosody deliberately and frequently. In the process, children get to hear prosodic adult reading and learn to reproduce it in their oral reading until it becomes natural for them too.

The primary elements of prosodic reading are:

- appropriate phrasing (clustering words as they belong together within sentences),
- pausing briefly (both within and between sentences),
- stressing certain words or phrases appropriate to context,
- rising and falling pitch (inflection) that matches the text (both within and at the end of sentences), and
- expressiveness that matches the context (for example, sounding horrified if something shocking has happened).

As we've seen, reading for both comprehension and prosody can't really kick in until children are decoding a piece of text with sufficient accuracy and automaticity. That's because they won't have any mental reserves free to think much about meaning or how the words hang together in syntactic units if they're still spending all their intellectual energy figuring out what each word is. Think again about early reading. Children are working out how to decode each word, saying it out loud (or in their heads) and then moving on to do the same thing with the next. Doing this for sentence after sentence is overwhelming if they haven't achieved the automaticity to read rapidly and effortlessly. Such halting reading will, of course, affect their rate, too, because it inevitably slows them down when they have trouble pronouncing each word and getting into the flow. Of course, this exhausting, word-level work affects a child's stamina for reading. And, of course, it makes understanding what you just labored through nearly impossible.

The really good news about reading fluency is that children can get better at reading something smoothly even within a single time period, say 20 minutes during one class. Their improvement will be palpable. They'll hear and feel that they've gone from halting word-by-word decoding to smooth, fluid reading. So will their teacher. This cycle of practice and success makes fluency work really rewarding. Doing this daily in second grade can be the key to locking in all the foundational skills learning that have come before. It sets every child on track to be successful readers for life.

Before you go on, write a quick summary of why prosody (prosodic reading) is an important indicator for teachers and parents to pay attention to:

The value of paying attention to prosodic (expressive) reading:

We'd say the answer to that question is that whether or not a child is reading with appropriate expression is a great window into whether or not she has good comprehension. And that information can be gathered a lot more quickly and less stressfully through listening to a child reading than through formal assessments. If a young reader's brain can attend to the meaning of what she reads to the degree that she can attend to *how* it should be read, it's a good signal that all reading systems are firing effectively.

Now we have that squared away, let's turn to the how to get it into classroom practice daily.

What Does Daily Fluency Practice Look Like?

There are just two ways to improve fluency. The research is wonderfully clear. Fluency is one of the most straightforward aspects of all literacy. One is for children to follow along with the text while a skilled reader reads it aloud. The second is to do repeated reading of the same passage[2] after hearing a fluent model of what that passage should sound like. That element of getting the text passage modeled skillfully is key. Repeatedly reading badly—mispronouncing words, getting the cadence all wrong, or blowing through punctuation—reinforces error patterns and dysfluency and is really discouraging. If the reader mispronounces words, she'll have no idea what she just read. Reading without meaning-making or success will quickly come to seem like a fruitless enterprise.

Children need skilled, solid models of what fluent reading sounds like. When they themselves are practicing, they need to know what the passage they're to be reading should sound like. After all, they need to do lots of fluency practice to get to that 50th percentile second-grade oral reading norm, so it had better feel good and be as fun as possible. All students need encouragement and positive reinforcement when they're being challenged.

[2] Note that "a passage" can be anything short enough for repeated reading within a period of 15 or so minutes! It can be an article, a poem, an important excerpt from something longer you're reading in class, procedures or directions, *anything* worth spending some time on!

There has been some confusion about wide reading versus repeated reading. We are major fans of wide reading—for growing children's vocabularies and their stores of knowledge—but not when the focus is on improving fluency! There was an Institute of Educational Sciences (the research division of the Department of Education) publication in their *What Works Clearinghouse Practice Guide for Foundational Skills* written in 2016 that is very clear about this:

> *In repeated reading, students are less likely to practice incorrect word reading or to guess unknown words. They are repeatedly exposed to the same words, which should help students recognize them more efficiently. Wide reading, on the other hand, exposes students to more diverse vocabulary and world knowledge. (Foorman et al., 2016)*

From a study by Schwanenflugel, Hamilton, Kuhn, Wisenbaker, and Stahl (2004):

> *Perhaps the best study of the development of prosodic features in children's oral reading to date is one by Dowhower (1987). Using audiotaped samples of students' reading, Dowhower studied the effect of repeated reading on oral reading prosody in second-grade children who showed adequate word decoding but who read in a slow, word-by-word way . . . She found that, after repeated practice, the children made fewer pauses not dictated by sentence structure . . .*

There are tried-and-true means to practice fluency. Here are four of the most common, all of which have a solid research base behind them.[3] Remember, all of these require that a fluent reader reads the passage first *while the children follow along* so they see how to pronounce the words and have that skilled model in their heads. There will be times you'll want to read more than once while children follow. This could be because the ideas you're reading about are so important, because the text is especially complex, or because there are lots of words you suspect your students may not know. It's important that each reading has a different purpose to it so your students stay engaged.

Echo Reading

Echo reading is very supportive of new or insecure readers. It takes the passage you're reading for fluency practice and chunks, or segments it, in contrast to choral reading, where the passage is read by the whole group together. In echo reading, you first read the whole passage with everyone following. Then you read a section of the text and stop so the children get a turn at reading the

[3] Paige, D., & Liben, D. D. *Building Reading Fluency*. Part 2 of a 2-part series *Aligned*. March 28, 2016.

same section (echoing your fluent model). This might be a sentence or two, a verse of a poem, or maybe even a full paragraph. You would go through the text you're using a couple times doing echo reading.

Choral Reading

Choral reading, as the name implies, is when the whole group reads the selection together after they follow along while the teacher (or a fluent volunteer) reads first. The first several readings of the fluency packet selection at Family Academy for each week always began with choral reading of the passage. You can also intersperse echo reading with choral reading to break things up.

Paired or Buddy Reading

Here, students are paired up. We like to pair a slightly stronger reader with a slightly less fluent reader and have the stronger reader go first as the model, but you know how to pair your students and should do what works best for your class. In any case, once the whole class hears the passage read fluently, the pairs take turns: one student reading aloud while the other listens and tracks in the text before swapping places. The listener always rereads what his partner just read before moving on to a fresh section.

Paired reading is a great time for you to move around and provide feedback and coaching. Children need to get clear and actionable feedback on how they are doing with fluency. They need their pronunciation corrected if they're mispronouncing words. They need to be coached on expressiveness and on how well they're reading punctuation—all the aspects of fluency that will make them successful. One of the benefits of giving feedback during paired reading is you get a "two-for-one" efficiency because the buddy reader is hearing you give the feedback and learning from it, too. And even better, often buddies learn to give one another useful feedback, too.

Repeated Reading

That simple research base consisting of just two practices is present in each of these systems. There is also simply engaging in repeated reading after hearing the fluent model. You can adapt this practice to all sorts of classroom communications. Having your children follow along while you read aloud important directions for an activity and then having two or three volunteers read them aloud again to cement them is a good use of just a couple minutes of time.

The same is true when children are reading and answering comprehension questions in a group. You should ask the child who answers a question to go back in the text, tell everyone where so they can go back too, and have her read the section aloud where she found her evidence. More prosaic, but important too! Practice rereading for announcements home you'd actually like to get communicated to the household adults. If you do quotes of the day in your room, a Morning Message, or any other valued rituals, those are perfect for quick fluency work. So are word problems in math or going over safety rules or the details of an upcoming field trip you want everyone to absorb. Anything that exists in writing can be used for fluency practice. In fact, practicing fluency with more everyday reading materials like these examples expands your children's repertoire of types of texts they're comfortable with. Always a good thing!

What are some easy ways you see to build fluency in your students (including things you already do)?

Fluency Packets (or Substitute Your Own Fun Daily Routines)

We centered our practice on our fluency packets because the passages were fun and the routine was easy, two valuable qualities with a vital reading skill we were determined to make sure every child got during the course of the year! We set up the fluency routines to incorporate the research-based approaches we just covered, as you'll see. The passages ranged from silly poems by people like Jack Prelutsky or Shel Silverstein to inspirational writing (excerpts from famous speeches, Civil Rights testimonials) to fables to song lyrics. Each summer, we would assemble the passages in a slim three-ring binder labeled, "The Fluency Packet," complete with a table of contents and pages for parents' initials. Each incoming second-grader got one. There was a weekly routine with the selection of the week with 15–20 minutes each day dedicated to fluency.

Here's how it generally worked. We stuck to a weekly system and had to adjust for short weeks of course, which we would sometimes do by using a shorter text that week. Six- or seven-day cycles are fine, too, whatever works for your setting. In general, we spent 15–20 minutes each day on fluency.

Day	Classwork	Homework
Monday	Passage is read aloud by the teacher a couple of times. Students follow. The teacher guides a discussion about what the meaning of the passage is and makes sure any new vocabulary has been introduced and defined. Then the students engage in several rounds each of echo and choral reading with the teacher actively coaching and correcting mispronunciations, paying attention to punctuation, and encouraging prosody. Once everyone has a sense of how the passage should be read, practice stops for the day (Mondays are the longest fluency day, perhaps 20–25 minutes).	Students read the passage aloud at home five times. Parents initial that oral reading was done.[4]
Tuesday	Passage is read aloud by the teacher once, echo read with students once. One-quarter of the class (the most fluent students) stands in front of the room, and one child after the other reads the passage aloud. The rest of the class follows along. Fluency packets are an option in literacy centers and during independent work time.	• Students read the passage aloud at home five times. • Parents initial reading was done and comment if they want to.
Wednesday	Passage is read aloud by the teacher once, echo read with students once. Second one-quarter of the class (next strongest group) reads the passage aloud one after the other. The other students follow along. Fluency packets are an option in literacy centers during independent work time.	• Students read the passage aloud at home five times. • Parents initial reading was done and comment if they want to.

(Continued)

[4] We found that fluency practice through the packets was matched only by multiplication-table memorizing for enthusiastic parent buy-in and support for home practice. It made total sense that their children would have to practice reading fluently to become fluent readers, and they understood how that connected to reading success. Because all they were attesting to by initialing was that their child had practiced, there was no barrier even for our parents who didn't speak or read English. There were many Family Academy homes around Central Harlem where second-graders could be spotted reading aloud to a caretaker for a few minutes every school night while the evening meal was being prepped.

Day	Classwork	Homework
Thursday	Passage is read by the teacher once, echo read with students once. The third group of students stands up front and reads the passage aloud one after the other. Other students follow along. Fluency packets are an option in literacy centers during independent work time.	• Students read the passage aloud at home five times. • Parents initial reading was done and comment if they want to.
Friday	Passage is read by the teacher once, echo read with students once. All remaining students stand up front and read the passage aloud one after the other. Other students follow along.	None

The daily fluency work was one of the students' favorite parts of the day, rivaled only by recess and teacher read-aloud in popularity. It was active for everyone, everyone had a role, and everyone knew what was required. The teachers would riff on the routine to make it more fun, especially during the later parts of each week when the repetition started to feel like too much. We dubbed these "enhancers," and the sky was the limit. We invited children to play with prosody by inventing or adopting different personas when it was their turn to read aloud. Read it like you're an old man! Rap the passage! Read it in an exaggerated accent. Read it as a witch might read it. Read it like you're a royal queen talking to your subjects or you're talking to a baby. Get with a friend and read it as a duet this week! Everyone loves these enhancers, no matter what setting we've worked in.

Think about the implications of this routine. By the end of each week, between the home practice and the multiple daily oral readings (while everyone else followed along in their own packet), that passage would have been heard, read, and followed something like 60 times in a class of 26 students. Plus, it meant that every child in our second grade performed for her peers at least once a week. Our students became poised public speakers from then on! The hams got to be hams; the quieter children got to build their confidence and be aware that they could do this. The less fluent children got to hear the passage modeled a lot before it was their turn to read, with the result that every student experienced a successful experience she associated with reading and felt herself a fluent, expressive reader each and every week. One other thing: Through our fluency program, our students understood that practicing makes you better, so they started to internalize the valuable lesson that practice pays off in improved skills and ability.

Do you see why reading fluency wasn't an issue at Family Academy? Why we said at the top of this chapter that it was way easier than systematic phonics work?

As you already know, we set aside this routine for a couple weeks three times a year to let the children prepare for a bigger public reading: this one with a party vibe and for an audience of their families and school adults. That event, as you read, was carefully prepared for, so every child experienced what it felt like to be successful at something valuable—reading—in front of people important in her life.

Assessing Reading Fluency

Informally assessing children's fluency is easy and has probably already jumped off the page at you. You're listening to these children weekly. You now know that prosody is a great indicator of whether or not students understand what they're reading. You're hearing children read individually, and you're hearing them within the chorus during choral reading so you know who keeps making miscues longer than others. You'll know who is fine to read the week's passage aloud fluently on Tuesday versus who needs until Friday to get in all that extra practice. And you'll anguish over who isn't improving even with all this weekly practice. Those children in that last bucket need to get quick and focused attention, possibly via a formal evaluation, because it's likely that something significant isn't working for their literacy development. Is their hearing okay (although that should have been addressed back in kindergarten at the latest because it would impact phonemic awareness big time)? Do they not have a well-developed sense of English phonics patterns they should have mastered, so they need significantly more support with those? Did they leave first grade without automaticity? If so, why? What is going on for that child?

Getting a precise and more formal measure of each child's fluency so you can see where she is on the Hasbrouck and Tindal scale is time consuming in most settings. If your school uses an early grades assessment protocol that includes a fluency screening, some system may already be in place. But if it isn't or you don't trust that screening, you'll need to make time to sit down with each of your students one on one at least twice each school year. You can, of course, train any paraprofessionals or classroom aides you have available to assist with fluency assessments too. There are suggestions for resources to use to do that in the sources section at the end of the chapter.

This is the last chapter that walks you through the different elements of foundational reading. These first six chapters have focused on these pivotal skills developing at the optimal times: during the developmental point in kindergarten through second grade where they belong. We laid our chapters out in that order. We've worked to make it clear what needs less time and can happen organically through modeling and reading aloud (concepts of print) and what needs the most careful planning and attention (systematic phonics). All of this work is in service to reading for understanding, knowledge, and pleasure, and those outcomes can't happen without all these pieces coming together successfully for a young reader. Each and every child we encounter deserves a future as a sturdy reader.

The final chapter of the book addresses what to do for the many children who didn't get what they needed in their primary education to become a solid reader. This was through no fault of their own, and we need to discuss what to do for all of them before we close.

Sources for Deeper Learning and Teaching

Fluency Packets and fluency resources from Achieve the Core

https://achievethecore.org/page/2756/fluency-resources

Tim Rasinski's Collection of resources

Inexpensive, all-you'll-need books to assess reading fluency (one for younger grades, one for older)

http://www.timrasinski.com/resources.html

Tim Rasinski's *Three Minute Reading Assessments* for grades one through four (Scholastic)

https://shop.scholastic.com/teachers-ecommerce/teacher/books/3-minute-reading-assessments-word-recognition-fluency-and-comprehension-grades-1-4-9780439650892.html

Works Consulted

Dowhower, S. L. (1987). Effects of repeated reading on second-grade transitional readers' fluency and comprehension. *Reading Research Quarterly*, *22*, 389–406.

Foorman, B., Beyler, N., Borradaile, K., Coyne, M., Denton, C. A., Dimino, J., . . . Wissel, S. (2016). *Foundational skills to support reading for understanding in kindergarten through 3rd grade* (NCEE 2016-4008). Washington, DC: National Center for Education Evaluation and Regional Assistance (NCEE), Institute of Education Sciences, US Department of Education. Retrieved from the NCEE website: http://whatworks.ed.gov

Hasbrouck, J. (2006). For students who are not yet fluent, silent reading is not the best use of classroom time. *American Educator*, *30*.

Hasbrouck, J., & Tindal, G. (2017). *An update to compiled ORF norms* (Technical Report No. 1702). Eugene, OR: Behavioral Research and Teaching, University of Oregon.

Liben, D., & Paige, D. D. (2016, October 16). *What is reading fluency?* [Web log post]. Retrieved from https://achievethecore.org/aligned/what-is-reading-fluency/

Liben, D., & Paige, D. D. (2016, October 28). *Building reading fluency.* [Web log post]. Retrieved from https://achievethecore.org/aligned/building-reading-fluency/

Rasinski, T. (2004). Creating fluent readers. *Educational Leadership*, *61*, 46–51.

Rasinski, T. V. (2010). *The fluent reader: Oral and silent reading strategies for building word recognition, fluency, and comprehension* (2nd edition). New York: Scholastic.

Rasinski, T., & Cheesman Smith, M. (2018). *The megabook of fluency.* New York: Scholastic (Winner of the 2019 Teachers' Choice Award for the classroom).

Schwanenflugel, P. J., Hamilton, A. M., Kuhn, M. R., Wisenbaker, J. M., & Stahl, S. A. (2004). Becoming a fluent reader: Reading skill and prosodic features in the oral reading of young readers. *Journal of Educational Psychology*, *96*, 119.

Chapter Seven

Unfinished Learning and Older Students: A Story

When our Family Academy students reached middle school age each year, we needed to bring in a good number of new students because New York City class size requirements expanded sharply for sixth grade. Our 20 new sixth-graders, among them a young man named Reggie, joined a group of about 45, largely made up of children who had been with us since kindergarten.

By that point, we had a well-tuned and coherent approach to reading instruction the teachers and we had created, and nearly all our "home-grown" students were real readers. That's not to say they all passed the annual reading tests at or above national norms, but they were all fluent and functional readers. That wasn't the case with Reggie or any of the newcomers, and we really needed to address their dire reading needs quickly so we wouldn't create some kind of awful ability grouped partitions within our tight-knit school community.

Reggie wasn't having it, which was a problem on several fronts, not the least of which was he was a natural leader. He was also a good athlete and was pretty sure he was headed to the NBA where annoying activities like reading wouldn't be factors in his life. Although we would be really happy for him if that dream were achieved, we also wanted a plan B in place. All of us in the school community had worked hard to make reading and academic achievement values in the school, and we didn't want Reggie's charisma to jeopardize that culture in the middle school, especially with so many new students to convince.

Reggie was really smart, but he'd put most of his brainpower into avoiding the fact that reading was a problem. So we launched our efforts on several levels. Our veteran parents, who had stuck with us through our early reading disasters and who had seen the benefits of what we had now, met in a series of orientations with the parents of the 20 new students, Reggie's mom among them. We met with them, too, to explain what we were going to do to address the fact that none of their children were on grade level in reading. And we were really honest with the new students. We named their reading challenges and promised that if we worked hard together they would improve.

There was no magic bullet here. Reggie resisted daily for a long time. But the veteran parents had convinced his mom to support the reading interventions we were introducing, and she made sure he stayed with us and tried, however grudgingly, most days. His new basketball coach leaned on Reggie, too, and made cooperation during the school day a condition for joining practices daily, which helped a lot too.

We had "literature groups" as a core part of the curriculum already, where students read trade literature, and these were grouped by reading ability. Reggie joined the other dozen or so students furthest behind in reading in their own group so they could have their reading needs addressed daily. We were honest with all of them about what they needed to do to get stronger (more on that later), and we concentrated on building up reading fluency and supporting their listening comprehension so they could learn as much as possible while they strove to strengthen their own reading abilities.

We asked our new dean of the middle school, Mr. Walker, to teach this group, and Mr. Angel, the gym teacher and basketball coach, often stuck his head in to check on Reggie and the other students. We worked closely with Mr. Walker to develop a system for the group that would improve outcomes. The group read a book, always, just as the other groups did, but Mr. Walker did most of the reading while they followed along in their copies. As with the other groups, we picked grade-level trade literature, both fiction and nonfiction we thought most of the students would like, and they engaged in vigorous discussions and did written work on the book. But every encounter with the book was also a carefully designed fluency strengthener. Following along while Mr. Walker read aloud was one. Having to find the place where evidence lay during the frequent discussions and reread sections to provide evidence for their answers was another. The other students had to go back in the book and follow along then, too, to see if they agreed with the position. But we also set aside 20 minutes daily for "prepared fluency practice," a no-nonsense middle school version of the fluency packet work the second-graders did daily. In this case, several paragraphs from their current book were assigned. After fluent modeling from Mr. Walker and some echo and choral reading, they had to work on that section on their own or with buddies to pass an end-of-week test. They had to read the assigned passage as perfectly as possible. Any mispronunciation, any overlooked punctuation, any poor chunking of parts of the sentence, any and all errors cost them five points off their starting point of a perfect 100. They were also given a holistic score for their prosody, or expressiveness, each week. They had to pass those performance tasks with a score greater than 85%, and these weekly scores were a big part of their grade. The demand, though grueling, was doable, and they all eventually came around to doing the work.

Reggie, happily, was able to translate the concept of practice making you better at skills into the reading work. Although he never jumped on the "reading is great" bandwagon, he eventually stopped working so hard at resisting and starting just doing the work. When the group read the fabulous *Holes*, around midwinter, he started getting perfect scores on his weekly prepared readings. Reggie's brain connected with solid intervention practice, and he made up a ton of ground that year in sixth grade.

In addition to the prepared readings, we also had all the new students doing 15 minutes of partnered fluency daily (a system of buddy reading we'll explain later), tapping into a bevy of volunteers from the school staff and community that Meredith coordinated in her role as head of the middle school. We've used partnered fluency in many other settings since, and it is always beautiful and effective. We'll describe how partnered fluency works when we get to naming the specifics of what you can do for your students who aren't reading well enough.

What we designed for our middle schoolers was simple and intense—and effective. Those new students reluctantly and gradually became fluent with grade-level material as did the groups that came in new every year after. Doing that hard work paid off, and they were able to see it for themselves. Once they became more fluent, they started to comprehend and recall what they'd read better. They started to feel better about themselves as students, too. This was all going on while we were folding these new students into a strong school culture. Our veteran students were willing to fold the newcomers in and helped them trust that the Family Academy was a supportive and nurturing place, one that took seriously the idea of the whole person.

The lessons those students taught us, refined and enhanced by knowing the research on bridging reading gaps and many other encounters with older students who couldn't read to their—or our—satisfaction, form the basis of this chapter.

There are broad consequences to being a student who can't read well. How many people have you met or known in your life who said in one form or another, "I'm not a 'math person,'" "I'm just not good in math," or something like that? It's not great that it seems okay to say that, yet somehow, it's acceptable. But turn to reading, and the taboos start. How many people have you heard say out loud, "I'm just not good at reading" or "I'm not a reading person"? A lot fewer, right? That's because saying you can't read is too much like saying you're stupid. Everyone knows that learning to read, above all, is what you come to school to do. So how are students who didn't learn to read supposed to feel? They don't feel good about themselves, and if they're older, they've hidden and avoided revealing their reading weakness for years. State tests and everything that swirls around them in our current school culture doesn't make this any better. These students feel crummy, and that feeling tends to extend to how they feel about their intellectual abilities.

Altering those feelings is part of our work too. You have to believe in your students' abilities for them until they see progress for themselves. Work with students who have unfinished business in reading is just as much about encouraging and cheerleading as it is about doing exactly the right things technically.

In every school we've worked in, every conference we've presented at, every educational gathering we've attended, the one universal question that's always asked is what to do about older students who are years behind in reading comprehension. It might be the most pervasive and frustrating problem in American education. And always, after some discussion, or in schools listening to students read, it becomes clear these students getting asked about are in virtually all cases disfluent.

This chapter is our answer to what you can do. We're assuming there are a couple different ways these different suggestions we offer can be used. You could incorporate them into a reading group in your classroom daily—as part of your instruction. That's essentially what we did with our new sixth-graders each year. We had reading groups at the same time for the whole grade so we could fold in extra adults like Mr. Walker and have smaller groups, by ability, for that one part of the day. So our intensive literature groups were part of all students' English Language Arts (ELA) experience daily. But these ideas could also be part of a tier two or even tier three intervention. It depends on your setting, what resources you have available, and your own ability to undertake these kinds of supports.

We also want to say plainly it's our position that weak oral fluency means weak comprehension. Repairing fluency isn't all there is to getting comprehension on track, but it's a lot of it. There's a ton of research (Chard, Vaughn, & Tyler, 2002; Fuchs, Fuchs, Hosp, & Jenkins, 2001; Jenkins, Fuchs, van den Broek, Espin, & Deno, 2003; Torgesen & Hudson, 2006) backing our position. So the interventions and approaches suggested in this chapter will all center on fluency work, along with coaching in pinpointed phonics patterns as a heavier form of intervention for any student who needs it.

We're emphasizing this as another pitch for prevention as much as for the solid research base. How much better is it to ensure strong reading *before* a child is labeled as a weak reader? To address issues as a school before they emerge?

How do you ensure this? By addressing fluency vigorously in second grade (where, as you've seen, children think it's actually fun and where it belongs developmentally!). We've sometimes seen poor oral fluency not addressed for younger students because people working with them don't believe oral fluency affects comprehension. It does.

Even if you're in repair mode because your students didn't come to you with a strong foundational reading experience, focusing on fluency is going to get your students a long way toward reading better. One last note: We're assuming you read the fluency chapter before you came here. If you didn't yet, you should go back so the discussion here makes sense.

- Disfluency is caused by weaknesses in the other foundational skills. In our experience as well as research (Torgesen & Hudson, 2006), students' poor fluency primarily reflects a lack of accuracy and automaticity in decoding. Either there are too many words students can't decode accurately or they take too long to do so. Either case causes dysfluency. In some cases, decoding and automaticity are so weak they need to be directly confronted. We'll discuss that in the second half of the chapter.
- There's really good news we've built this chapter around. That is, in *many* cases, those weaknesses can be strengthened by fluency work alone, perhaps with some pinpointed coaching when you spot obvious gaps in phonetic knowledge (for example, when you realize a student doesn't know that "-tion" is always pronounced /shun/ and you point it out). That's the good news portion of this chapter, and we'll take it first.
- To catch up, students need to work with and become fluent with texts they actually need to read for school. So instruction should be with texts at grade level (Paige, 2006, 2011; Stahl & Heuback, 2005; Young & Bowers, 1995) and, to keep things simple, with what you're already using in your lessons whenever possible. That's easier for you (or whoever is working with your struggling readers) and obviously more useful to your students.
- If students are extremely far behind and you feel you just can't, the texts can either be shortened so all students are still accessing the same grade-level material, or you should substitute reading selections that are as close to grade level as possible. Students need to strengthen their automatic decoding during fluency work, so the weaker they are, the more repetition they'll require before they can fluidly read any given passage. They need to read connected, meaningful text and learn how to parse phrases within sentences and pay attention to punctuation within and between sentences along with decoding. Because they're older, and behind, they need to do it all at once. It's worth lingering on these components for a moment because it explains why it is so hard to catch older students up. They likely need some decoding instruction if there are phonics patterns they haven't mastered. Then they need *lots* of practice to achieve greater accuracy and automaticity. They'll likely need more repetitions to achieve this than other students who already (perhaps years earlier) picked up those patterns and learned them to the point of automaticity. After second or third grade, text is more complex. That means there are more infrequent words in their grade-level texts.

That makes it even more difficult to achieve accuracy and automaticity because these words, being infrequent, will be less likely to repeat.

- Students need to be able to read grade-level text, which in many cases they have not been exposed to, perhaps ever, if they've always been instructed in leveled reading groups. And all this is going on while students are trying to learn what's being taught in the grade they're currently in. That is true even though they didn't get full advantage of the learning opportunities in earlier grades because they couldn't read what other children were able to.

That list contained a lot of obstacles for older students who have unfinished foundational skills learning! This is why the problem is so pervasive and extensive. The higher the grade, the more pernicious the problem.

Addressing reading fluency is the key to catch these students up. But recall for a minute how badly people who can't read well tend to feel about reading and about themselves. Years of frustration and failure have led to avoiding reading as much as possible—especially the humiliation of reading aloud. Reading is associated with failure and feeling stupid. The last thing these students, being, in fact, so smart they've been getting by on their wits, are going to want to do is read aloud daily with you! You have to get them to trust that they can improve and that you believe in their ability to do so. You may have to do *all* the believing for a while, loud and clear.

Here's what we've done about that and what we counsel you to do before you start an upper-grades fluency program. It'll take about 30 minutes. It really helped us with Reggie (and his mom), and it is a vital step.

- Bring the students you're targeting for support together in a private space. Ask each of them to read aloud a *very* short grade-level paragraph, depending on factors like your standing relationships, student age level, and current degree of trust, which might be to you in private (or possibly in front of their peers), to another available adult, or to each other. There generally can be resistance to doing this, but it's important. So if all of those alternatives feel like too much, ask them to read it to themselves in a whisper voice no one but themselves can hear.

- Follow this by asking how that went. Usually, you'll get a pretty honest response, but if not, with a little friendly prodding most will admit it wasn't great.

- Then read the same paragraph out loud twice, with students following along.

- Then describe echo reads quickly (you read a sentence, they echo the same sentence back to you as a group and so on through the paragraph), and then do two echo reads.

- Then do two choral reads (same thing, but the whole paragraph gets read in one go).
- Then ask students to read it to each other in pairs one more time.
- Then stop and ask how the paired reading went. They always say it was better. If things feel relaxed and loose, ask if anyone wants to read the paragraph aloud.
- Then, ask if, in the last 20 minutes, they got smarter. If not how could they suddenly read this grade-level text so much better?

Of course, they'll know they didn't suddenly grow smarter. Tell them what they did improve was their reading fluency for that passage (be sure to define what you mean by that: smooth and errorless reading, like a river flowing). Explain they got more fluent because they practiced, and the problem they're having with reading is they lack reading fluency. So the hard work of trying to pronounce and recognize the words and read them in sentences one after another is taking up all their mental energy. That leaves them no energy to think about what the text is saying, so their comprehension isn't kicking in for them the way it should, and reading gives them no payoff.

After this, you need to explain that fluency has absolutely nothing to do with intelligence. Fluency ability resides in a completely different part of the brain than the places that house intelligence, and fluency ability is like a muscle that can get stronger quickly if exercised. Finish off with the notion that fluency, as with dribbling a soccer ball or playing an instrument, gets better with practice, practice, practice. And the practice we're talking about is working just like we did today, with what they are supposed to read for class or other materials, and with enough regular practice, their fluency will start to improve very quickly—in a matter of months and not years.

You'll have to do a version of this talk with the parents of these students too, as we did for Reggie's mom and our other new parents. They deserve to know all this information, and of course, they need to know what you're planning to do with their children!

Disfluency is not only at the base of struggling reader's problems, but it is also integral to students' social and emotional well-being as well. How do students feel good about themselves if they think they aren't smart, if they know year in and year out they are reading simpler books than the rest of the class, if they know there's no way they'll do well on the test everybody talks and worries about every year? If the problem remains unaddressed year after year until they go to high school, it gets worse by their being placed in a lower track. This is the reality for millions of American students.

We've been aware of the damage caused by not getting early reading right, and obsessing over it has fueled our work for decades. Remember our first group at the Family Academy? That happened in 1994. But we keep getting reminders that we educators still aren't doing a good job addressing the reading needs of all children.

We got a good dose of the power of that reality to do harm a few years ago working with a group of suburban eighth-graders. Throughout the entire half hour of the "Experiencing Fluency" interaction we just walked you through, there was one tall eighth-grade boy who we knew was very popular. He wasn't having it. Other than the buddy reading time, he was lying prone on one of the tables in the corner of the room. At the end, when we wrapped up and talked about how fluency worked and how it could be improved, he sat up and announced, "That all makes sense. It's exactly what I need. But I'm not gonna do it," and lay back down. This student had already staked his self-image and position in school as being a nonreader and academic outsider so strongly, in his mind there was no turning back.

How does a student arrive at this point? Students don't generally go through our schools without being noticed. They go through our schools without being *helped* because too often schools don't know what to do. There are interventions, *expensive* interventions, but they don't address the problem properly. For starters, interventions can't address the social and emotional underpinnings of the problem or the massive toll it takes on older students. This gets worse the older students are. Perhaps the best evidence for this is a student who succeeded *despite* being disfluent.

A while ago, I (David) worked closely with teachers for a year in a suburban high school. In the late spring, one of the English teachers approached me about coming in as a guest speaker to her advanced placement (AP) class. She noted that my work with them in many ways had been a course on the psychology of reading, and she thought it would be interesting for her AP students to hear a mini-version of what I'd taught their teachers. I agreed and thought it would be great fun. At the end of my talk, which included a lot on foundational skills but also touched on reading comprehension and how it's influenced by vocabulary, syntax, motivation, and knowledge challenges, Robert, one of the students in the AP class, came up to me, introduced himself, and said, "Mr. Liben, I think I have a fluency problem." To which I replied, something to the effect of "Robert, you're in AP English, how could that be?" And I asked what college he was going to and Robert said "Oberlin." That's where Meredith went, and I knew it wasn't that easy to get into. As I was starting on yet more skeptical questions, Robert politely stopped me and said, "You don't understand. I spend as long as six *hours every* night on my homework." I soon found out Robert's parent taught in the district. His own quiet grit and compensations had evidently left Robert on his own. On the spot, and flustered, all I could come up with was that for the summer he get audio and physical copies of books that he thought would set him up well at Oberlin, any genre or topic he wanted, but written at an adult level, and listen while following along to build his fluency with college-level texts. Clearly, he was a motivated student, so I suggested he take the same 6 hours he was currently giving his homework and use it in this way. That fall, Robert's AP teacher forwarded me a note from him, in which he told her he was spending less time reading for his first-semester classes at Oberlin than he had in high school. Since then, I've recommended this as a technique for some other highly motivated high school students. They are, alas, far and few between. Being stuck being disfluent for years is just too much of a soul-crushing barrier.

So what can we do to address this problem and change academic trajectories for all those students who are struggling with reading? Before we go any further, gather your thoughts below.

What "Reggies" or "Roberts" do you have in your past or present? Do you know what, specifically, they're struggling with? How does it manifest itself in their feelings about school, about themselves, their hopes and plans for their future? If your student is from past years, do you know what she or he is up to now?

Two Types of Student Needs, Two Approaches to Repairing Reading Problems

We're dividing the answer to how to do this work into two parts.

First, we're going to focus on repairing fluency, with minor, "just-in-time" phonics support and coaching on how syllables work based on what you see the students you're working with stumbling over. Whom are you going to work with here? Cast back to the fluency chapter and think about those students who are reading below the 40th percentile rates on the Hasbrouck and Tindal norms for the time of year and grade level you're with (Hock et al., 2009). If you don't have access to fluency data for your students, these would be the students who you know are disfluent—your reluctant readers.

It may be that focusing on fluency is all you can manage in the course of your other teaching responsibilities, so this first section may be one you stay with and utilize. But it may be you have access to good digital programs and can do a variety of interventions without neglecting all your other responsibilities. Ideally, your other students (those who are below the 20th percentile in reading fluency) would have support in a tier two or three intervention. But believe us, it will help your students a lot if you can implement many of these fluency improvements we outline in the following. These interventions would be considered tier two interventions, although several of them might be moves you find you can easily slip into your regular (tier one) classroom teaching once you heighten your awareness of the many opportunities to do so. For many of your students, this will be enough. You and they will see what feel like radical improvements.

But it won't be enough for everyone. So second, we're going to focus on more intensive repair work: finding ways to practice phonics patterns students never mastered that are keeping them from achieving the automaticity they're lacking. This work would need to be done in small, pinpointed groups. It would need to be done in addition to the fluency work we're about to describe. It could be this work happens as an intervention outside of your classroom, and you concentrate on the fluency intervention. Or, if you're in a position to group your students for reading instruction, or you already do group, you may want to gather the students with the most unfinished foundational skills learning and work with them as one group within your class. Ideally, you could do something like we did at the Family Academy. We always had reading groups at the same time for all the students in a grade, so any extra adults available could push in and take small, ability-based groups for reading work. Just know that students who lack phonics knowledge need that support to catch up.

These two approaches can theoretically be done with any students from grades four through 12, but as you know, the higher the grade, the more time students have had to fall behind and the more alienated from school and reading they've become. So it's going to be harder in middle school and *far* harder in high school although *not* impossible. We've shared some good-news stories with you and have one more from Meredith's high school work coming.

Focusing on Fluency

The basic approaches to fluency here are the same as in the last chapter but adjusted upward to match the grade your students are currently in. The science of improving fluency doesn't change for any grade, but the texts students need to read will have more sophisticated vocabulary and syntax than primary-grade books. They'll also require greater background knowledge than texts students read in kindergarten to second grade. These issues will need to be addressed alongside fluency because students need to understand what they read. They always need to keep their eyes on the prize of comprehension. It's always the goal. Fluency is just an important stage on the road to independent reading comprehension.

You need to know your students' vocabulary and general knowledge are very likely not at grade level either because vocabulary and knowledge grow most efficiently with reading. Your disfluent students have read less in general and read less rich, complex text. Because many of them have become alienated from reading, they likely check out and understand less of what they read even when they're reading simpler texts.

The other difference with fluency work after second grade, an important one, is that you'll have to integrate some phonics instruction into the work. This will be that just-in-time phonics work mentioned before, and it's coming up because students get stuck not knowing how to decode a given pattern or not knowing how a word can be broken into syllables to help figure out how to pronounce it. These just-in-time interventions are powerful because each reinforces the fluency work and vice versa. Older students tend to be pretty efficient learners once they're bought in. *If* they have a grasp on most phonics and syllable patterns, it isn't so hard to pick up the rest because they've spent years in school hearing and seeing words. This efficiency is important to capitalize on in catching students up. It is one of the few things that might be a support even though they've gone years without gaining proficiency and ease in reading. Third- and fourth-grade students and, of course, students who have another language they're proficient in other than English, may not have as much of this familiarity to draw on.

Threaded throughout all these suggestions and stories of what we've done is our assumption that you're going to take our approaches and adjust them to fit your students' needs and your situation. That is as it should be, and we want to assure you we hope that's what will happen!

So here we go.

First, we'll show you a protocol to build comprehension while improving reading fluency. It can be used anytime you need students to learn from text. It's time consuming and may seem elaborate, but pay attention to how *many* different types of learning are in play as you read. We're assuming this would happen over the course of days, but that would depend on how long and elaborate the text is you're using.

- If at all possible, use texts students are reading in their regular (tier one) ELA or any other subject area classes, especially if these are at grade level. This will support students in their learning of the subject matter and will feel efficient to them and less like they're doing double work. The familiarity they have with the topic and the text from their fluency work will help build confidence when they're with their peers and interacting with the material as well. If for some reason you can't use what you already are teaching, then you should find texts online or in your library that are at or nearly at grade level and closely related to what students are reading in ELA, social studies, or science classes.

- Initial read-aloud to model fluent reading. Be sure to have students follow along, but let them use a pointer other than their finger: a closed pen or the eraser end of a pencil, perhaps an old piece of acetate cut into strips with highlighter tape to be a place-keeper. Older students are sensitive to feeling babyish, and not being able to read well already makes them feel bad enough. So be sensitive to this, but insist they follow along whenever you (or anyone) reads aloud. It isn't breaktime; it is the crucial work. Weak readers are accustomed to just listening.

  Explain why they have to follow along—always explain all of this! The truth is, they can use their listening comprehension to learn a lot when you read. That's been their primary mode for years. So remind them this work is to improve their fluency so they can access the text without you.

  Also, tell students that after this first read you are going to ask them what was going on in the text to remind them they're accountable for understanding as they follow along. The purpose of the initial read is to hear a fluent model, but the purpose of reading is to understand what you read. You don't want to lose sight of that. Fluency isn't the destination on this journey. It's the conduit.

- Second read-aloud. This time, tell students you'll be reading much more slowly and pausing every few sentences for them to circle any words they don't know. Be sure they follow along again. If you can't let them write on the page, they should write down words they don't know on a separate paper or in a notebook kept for this.

- Cold call (meaning, don't pick volunteers) students to spell out (just in case they can't pronounce a word) or read you words (if they can) they noted as not knowing. Go over each unfamiliar word by giving a quick, student-friendly explanation of each word. These explanations should be less than one minute because the context of the text read twice already will contribute to understanding many words from context—a valuable asset for your readers to discover (Biemiller, 2009). The exception, where you should spend time, are any words you think are essential to understanding the text. These words should get more time. You can do that by adding two sentences to your kid-friendly explanation; first, use the word in the same context as the text you are reading and, second, use a different context.

For example, if the word is *absolutely* and the sentence in the text is: *Studying that way, you'll learn absolutely nothing.* The kid-friendly explanation would be something like, "absolutely means completely, totally; so here he is saying you will learn nothing, not a thing. You won't learn just a little; you'll learn nothing at all." And then provide a sentence in a different context: *I know absolutely that we'll have fun on our field trip.* Very briefly explain what it means in this sentence.

- Hand out a series of questions that were prepared in advance. These should be text-dependent questions, meaning questions that can only be answered by reading the text, and it is perfectly fine to use the questions provided in your instructional materials. Read the questions aloud while students follow along and be sure they understand them.

- Tell students you are going to read the text once more while they follow along. This time when you pause, students should annotate in some way (or take quick notes on paper) what sections of the text answer or help answer any of the questions. Try as much as possible to have the order of the questions parallel the order answers will materialize in the text, and put any theme or main idea kinds of questions at the end. As you know from the last chapter, multiple readings are essential to growing fluency, and these students will need a lot of "multiples," but students will not just keep rereading, they need to have a different purpose for each read.

  Disfluent readers tend to be disfluent writers because they don't have the spelling patterns automated to capture their thoughts and ideas quickly. This adds to the general frustration. So you'll need to show them simple, efficient ways to annotate text while you build up those automatic patterns. For this same reason, you'll notice our recommendations tend to minimize how much we ask older struggling readers to write. We want them to focus on the reading demands and don't want to overload them.

- Put the students in pairs to answer the questions in writing. The pairs should be relatively homogeneous. Keep in mind that you yourself can partner with the weakest pairs during this time although being free to circulate is invaluable too. Periodically ask for answers to be in writing so students get a chance to improve their writing skills alongside their reading and here, too, be sure to tell students you'll cold call them to answer the questions. Whenever students answer a question, they should read aloud the portion or portions of the text they used to arrive at their answers. The rest of the group should find that place and follow along, too. This reinforces the idea of using evidence from the text while providing yet another swing through the text.

- Once all this is done, parts of the text should be used for reading aloud with expression or prosody. This time, pick a portion of the text and model reading it with expression while students listen. This one time, they *don't* follow along in the text. This is so they can concentrate on reading with expression. Follow this with having them do either an echo read or a choral read, depending on how much support you think they need at this point. Once you feel most or all students are reading with at least some degree of smoothness and expression, put them in pairs to do buddy reading. This is the *absolute* best time to see how students are doing with fluency and to provide feedback. This feedback is essential and can't be done as well in a larger group or even a small group. Students who are routinely struggling after all of these reads may need a referral for evaluation for special services or be considered for more intensive intervention such as the one we'll explore next.

  But before doing anything like that, we recommend trying to find some time to do one-on-one work with these students and, of course, bringing in parents to explain the concerns and how they can provide more support at home if possible. That being said, we believe there will be very few students who will not respond to this instruction.

At this point, you may be looking for some sort of culminating assignment that integrates or synthesizes the learning from the text. If you're using texts and questions from your curriculum, there may well be something like this provided. We don't recommend doing it with these students until they've achieved fluency and feel good about themselves as readers. That's simply because time is a precious commodity in schools. These types of assignments, as worthy as they are, won't improve fluency or automaticity. Keep your eye on the prize. If you can gain a classroom full of fluent students who missed a few culminating assignments during the year, wouldn't you take that trade-off? Wouldn't your students? Of course, if they have to do it as part of the curriculum or you're held accountable to do everything, you'll need to. But be as efficient as you can be.

This *isn't* to say you should rush through the exploration of text or shouldn't take questions or reflections from your students as they learn to read with confidence and how to study a text this carefully. It's *always essential* that students understand and appreciate what they are reading. But developing fluency with grade-level text is the core of this protocol, and without fluency, their future progress as independent, competent readers is compromised.

This protocol is designed to grow students' fluency with grade-level text while supporting their work and learning with your core instruction. These practices all align well with the research base on improving fluency and align well with standards-based teaching, too. But they aren't a rulebook. Remember to make adjustments to fit your situation and the students you're working with!

Beyond the intensive protocol we just described, there are other fluency interventions you can set up. Some are straightforward and simple, some more involved. We offer them to you, in addition to the others from the last chapter, so you can figure out what works best in your setting to make disfluency a problem of the past for your students.

Partnered Fluency

Remember our new middle schoolers who came in as disfluent readers? The other thing we did daily with them was this partnered fluency program for 15 minutes a day. This is really intended as a schoolwide intervention, to come together and erase disfluency as a problem once and for all. If you can convince your colleagues and school leaders to embark on a partnered fluency program across your school, you won't be sorry!

Students who can work together sympathetically and who read at similar levels are paired. We frequently tried to cross gender lines and even grade levels in making our pairs and actively avoided pairing children who were close friends. That was because we wanted the partnership to be about helping each other get fluent and doing so as unselfconsciously as possible. The adult in charge can be drawn from any number of sources: parent or community volunteer, front office staff, lunchroom or custodial staff, school aides and paraprofessionals, student teachers, or even interns and high school students.

No special setting is needed: among other places, we always did fluency work in isolated parts of the hall so that adult presence throughout the building was extended, and student passers-by maintained a respectful and appropriate noise level. Our fluency work doubled as hall monitoring. It also said loud and clear that literacy for all was valued in our school.

Pairs come out of their various classroom for a total of 15 minutes daily for their fluency work, and the adult volunteers work with as many pairs as they can. The adult coach is usually provided an appropriate text by the classroom teacher or could keep a file of articles for the pair that are of high interest to them both and grade-level appropriate. You could also use a fluency packet, either a free one listed in the resources or a fun one you make for each grade as a teacher professional development project. We used a mix of genres: poems, nonfiction, interesting newspaper articles, commercial passages, and famous speeches.

The student pairs only work on a paragraph or two a day, so gathering material is not very difficult. The coach has three copies of the day's passage prepared so that the readers and the coach all have their own copies.

The coach's role is to support the reading, keep time, give cues and strategies, point out unknown phonics or syllable patterns, remind the reader to attend to punctuation and overlooked syntax, and encourage but not to supply answers or let the student reading off the hot seat by taking over in any way to provide a break. The improvement comes through the hard work of the student reading aloud. The break comes when their partner takes over or the session ends. The work must be theirs.

One student reads first. She works intensively on decoding and reading accurately, word by word, punctuation included. The active reader has to get every word and punctuation mark right, even if she only makes it through one or two sentences. The other student follows her partner's work in a highly focused way. This is monitored by the coach's insistence that both students have a finger or a pencil pointed at the word the active reader is focused on.

The "resting" reader is not at full tension, but she should be paying close attention so she gets the full benefit of the hard work her partner is doing and the cues the coach is providing (so long as she is following along faithfully).

After the first reader has worked through a chunk of text for three or four minutes, generally a paragraph or two, the coach stops her. She then goes back to the beginning of the passage to read it fluently, *starting over* if she miscues. It's crucial for each reader to have, each and every day, a fluent reading experience before she stops. This is far more important than how much she reads. A single sentence read with fluency and expression is better than half a page read with mispronunciations and lack of expression. The point here is to break those patterns and let students experience smooth, fluent reading. For the fluent reading, too, the resting partner moves her finger to keep pace with the reader, and the coach continues to monitor. Once a fluent reading is achieved, the coach gets to praise lavishly while the student catches her breath and starts to relax. This is incredibly hard, brave work, and that needs to be acknowledged frequently and genuinely.

The partners then switch roles so that the first reader can rest (but still follow) while her partner does the hard work with the next section of the text. The coach continues to demand persistence on accurate word decoding, careful attention to punctuation, and perfection on the final, fluent rereading. In general, the 15 minutes is most fruitful if both readers get two chances to be the oral reader, and two chances to read silently while following along. But the time flies, and transitions take time.

We believed this 15 minutes daily of fluency work was more important to a student's academic success than any other activity he might miss while out of class for that short time. But it's good not to have the partnered reading at a time when one of the students might be missing a favorite activity, like gym, music, or recess. It was our experience that students appreciated the close attention of a different adult and saw the benefit of the fluency work. They almost always engaged in it willingly in more than one school we worked in. That good will shouldn't be jeopardized by asking them to miss their favorite part of the day.

We recommend partnered fluency be done at least four days a week for the full 15 minutes. If partnered fluency practice is kept up diligently, that is an hour of intense and focused practice weekly. If this is achieved, coaches and students alike will see the results of their work quickly, within just a few weeks! They'll continue to see improvements week by week as long as the system is followed consistently. This means students can "graduate" out of partnered fluency fairly rapidly, disfluency issue solved, which makes it a rare intervention indeed.

I (Meredith) was the sole English teacher in a Regional Career and Technical Center in rural Vermont. There, I got to work with every instructor to design coursework that was embedded in the content the program teachers needed their students to master. The students were all 11- and 12th-graders who took a year away from one of six area high schools to enroll in a full-day program of their choice. These programs covered a wide range of technical subjects: criminal justice, diesel technologies, graphic design, and building trades were just a few.

I'd joke with the students that I was the very teacher they'd come there to escape, and that was pretty much the case. They were there for their chosen technical program, not for the marvels of English. In most cases, they'd also come there to escape the frustrations of daily encounters with academic settings where they'd spent years having to confront their weak reading daily. *Every* year, between two-thirds and three-quarters of the incoming student body was disfluent.

This alarmed the instructors as much as it did me. The students wouldn't succeed in these trades without more functional literacy than many of them had. Career and Technical Education (CTE) instructors are almost all career changers who have years, if not decades, in their trades. They know what's required for success. Fortunately, I had a marvelous Director in Bill Sugarman, and the technical instructors were terrific colleagues. Those kids were *lucky* to spend all day with them. The program instructors all backed me in working with their students to address the epidemic of disfluency, and Bill allowed me to craft my schedule so I could screen every student every fall and then work with priority groups in turn over the course of the year to address fluency.

A word on that screening: I used the free ninth- to 12th-grade passages that Tim Rasinski had developed with the Ohio Literacy Alliance (there is a link to them in the resources section at the end; Dr. Rasinski is an uncommon researcher who constantly created practical tools for classroom teachers during his long career). Every student came to me for five minutes during the first couple weeks of school. I explained what I was asking them to do and why and promised that I would tell them the results and what they meant before they got up from the chair and walked back to their program. I *never* had a student refuse to cooperate, even though reading out loud for a minute to a new adult was excruciating to most of them. I think my promise to tell them how they did was the reason. Possibly for the first time in their lives in school, they were directly getting the results of an assessment themselves and getting an explanation of what it meant and what they could do to change it. It was empowering enough to keep them in their seats for the five minutes. I knew, de facto, as 16- to 18-year-olds they were in charge of their own reading futures, so I *had* to enlist them, but they did clearly appreciate that respect.

I folded the protocol you read about previously into my class sessions as frequently as possible, and we also set up a schoolwide partnered fluency program. We just asked each student involved to commit to partnered fluency for 15 minutes a day, four days a week for six weeks, and then they and I would evaluate how they were doing. They would either cycle out at that point or agree to do another six weeks. It was their choice. Students weren't happy about any of this for the most part, but their beloved instructors kept pressure on them to comply, and they mostly did. Adults came out of the woodwork to volunteer to coach pairs. Those students' hard work and willingness to try again even after all those frustrating years paid off with improved outcomes for many, even at the tail end of their kindergarten to 12th-grade educations.

The other alternative to a fluency packet wouldn't have been suitable for my CTE students. They wanted to spend most of their time in the shops learning what they'd come to the Center to do and would have revolted. As 11th- and 12th-graders, they were much older than students usually are who are targeted for fluency intervention. I needed to respect and acknowledge their own agency in the work at every intersection. If they were spending all day in academic subject classes, it would've been a different story. The fluency passages could have easily supported learning whatever topics were being studied in science, social studies, or English.

But the fluency packet is a great tool, and we hope you'll consider adopting it for your students.

Grades-Level Fluency Packets

A grade-level fluency packet, which works just as the second-grade version described last chapter, is essential for improving fluency for many reasons.

- Not only does it offer a handy way to address fluency daily, but each student's reading the text aloud to the group at the end of the week is a powerful motivator in two important ways.
    - It's a weekly chance for students to engage in public speaking and get comfortable with doing so. Public speaking is included in any set of state standards because it's so essential in many careers and in life. Yet it's really hard to find the time to devote to public speaking. If it's a "two-for-one" benefit along with improving fluency, how great is that?
    - Second, reading aloud fluently to your classmates with expression builds confidence and starts to erase feelings of intellectual inadequacy that built up over the years along with reading failure. Rebuilding confidence and self-efficacy is one of the most powerful parts of what you're trying to do with repairing reading problems. The older and further behind the student, the more important that goal is.
- If you set up your fluency packet protocol by bringing in parents (which you should always do with fluency interventions!), much of the practice work gets done at home.
    - There are premade fluency packets that also have recorded readers for each passage in the resource section at the end of the chapter. But you can also make your own to match topics in your curriculum or just to be more fun and inspiring for students.
- Prosody, reading aloud with expression that matches the text, is an important part of fluency. It has an interesting relationship with both fluency and comprehension. It's difficult to read with the appropriate expression and cadence if you don't understand what you're reading. Flipping the equation, reading with prosody actually strengthens comprehension. The reader starts to learn where to emphasize and where not, how sentences flow from clause to clause (the cadence of the text), when to raise her voice, and when to pause for emphasis. For this reason, prosody is best addressed and evaluated with the fluency packet passages. Because students spend about a week with each text, they should understand what they're reading!
- The fluency packet is the best way to harness time at home for practice. It's straightforward to explain to parents to elicit their support. With older students, out-of-school practice is more likely to happen if you can somehow enhance the practice through the use of technology. See if students would rather video themselves reading the text and then send it to you so they could replay it on the smartboard or a projector when it's their turn to read. If you're working with upper-elementary

students, the silly enhancers we discussed in the fluency chapter might be enough to get them to practice at home. Again, you'll know best for your students and setting!

So we're done with the first part of our system, which addresses foundational gaps primarily through fluency and will catch the majority of struggling readers. But you'll remember the root of fluency problems is a lack of automaticity in decoding. If automaticity and knowledge of phonics patterns are largely absent, solving that problem is where we're heading next.

Remember, the good news is the relationship between fluency and decoding is reciprocal. Instruction in fluency improves both the accuracy and automaticity of decoding; instruction in decoding improves fluency. The students we're trying to help in this next section need both. That they've never had enough exposure and practice with either is why they're in this boat, through no fault of their own. Our failure to provide adequate exposure and practice opportunities within so many interventions has failed our students in droves.

It's time to fix that.

Addressing Automaticity in Decoding with Fluency

For this part of the work, we're recommending you locate online resources put out by Kathy Ganske, the author of the solid *Word Journeys*. That will give you a scope and sequence for the work, diagnostic assessments so you know where your students need to start, and resources, such as lots of word lists grouped by pattern, for everything we discuss here. Ganske's book can give you support for your work with older students beyond what we can in this one chapter.

Ganske divides phonics patterns, which she calls features, into four stages reflecting progressive increases in decoding skill. They're described in chapter 2 of her book. These are Letter Naming, Within Word, Syllable Juncture, and Derivational Consistency. At this point, it would be helpful to read her first two chapters, especially if you aren't familiar with this level of phonic specificity. If you know or have worked with *Words Their Way*, it's based on this same work by Ganske. But if you can't pull yourself away from us or aren't sure about the investment, we understand completely and will give you as clear and quick a sense of this as we can here. We've also put some links to resources that address these same ideas in shorter, less elaborate ways than Ganske's comprehensive book does. They're in the resources section at the end of the chapter.

Ganske approaches phonics through spelling. You'll see that makes sense. Spelling is the mirror image of decoding, and as we said way back in chapter 5 on teaching structured phonics, spelling is the best assessment for how sturdy a young reader's mastery of decoding is. Words that students spell correctly can be read accurately and probably automatically; conversely, students can spell words they can read accurately and automatically. There are a *lot* of reciprocal relationships in reading, and it's good to take advantage of them whenever possible.

To embed phonics in your work with your struggling readers, you'll need to know what phonics patterns to address over time. David Paige's research, discussed in chapter 4 and linked in the works cited, found 70% of the large third-grade sample of students who had mastered Ganske's Within Word Stage (WWS) of decoding and read grade-level text with fluency passed the third-grade state assessment. In other words, if students' decoding skills were past the WWS level and they were fluent with third-grade-level texts, then they passed the third-grade reading test in large numbers. In personal communication, David Paige noted that students who have mastered WWS decoding will benefit going forward from a strong fluency program alone. Those are your students who will thrive quickly in the first set of protocols we laid out earlier.

This is important to know. Getting your students automatic with phonics patterns through the WWS should be your focus when you're working to fill in incomplete learning for your readers who are behind. You *can't* go back and do everything children should have learned in kindergarten through second grade. So it's really good news you don't have to. There's more (sort of) good news: Although systematic phonics instruction, as noted in chapter 4, has an extremely strong research base for kindergarten through second-grade instruction, it doesn't appear to be as strong an instructional approach for older students. So starting with basic, basic phonics isn't the way for you to go with your students.

This makes sense. Older students need to know they are doing real reading and making up ground toward the grade they're actually in. They also need to see their progress. Fluency practice provides both real reading and rapid, apparent progress. Students working hard to improve fluency can *feel* the results in a short period of time.

One way to determine where to start is to administer the Developmental Spelling Analysis (DSA), available online in a link included in the resources

---

[1] Digraphs are when two (or more) letters make one sound. You can have consonant digraphs (for example, /ch/, /ck/, /wh/, /tch/) or vowel digraphs, too (for example, /ea/, /oo/, /ay/).

[2] Affricates are the "breathy" letters: 'g,' 'j,' and 'h.' Say them to yourself while staying conscious of your mouth and breath, and you'll see that you first stop your breath then exhale pretty forcefully when you make these sounds.

section, and explained in chapter 3 of *Word Journeys*. The process is clear, and we'd recommend using the *brief* version. It takes very little time and will give you a clear picture of where the students you're working with are in this developmental progression.

In elementary school, most of your students would likely place in the Letter Naming stage, in middle school you will have some in the Within Word stage. Once you figure out where most of the students you're supporting are currently, we recommend you start one level *below* where most of your students did well on. Ganske calls this "dropping back" to give everybody confidence to begin with, and it makes sense to review quickly and then start in on the unfinished learning.

The Letter Naming stage contains the following phonics patterns (remember Ganske calls these "features" or "letter features"): initial and final consonants, initial and final consonant blends and digraphs,[1] short vowels, affricates,[2] final consonant blends, and vowel digraphs (in that order).

So, for example, if based on the DSA, all or nearly all of the students in your group are proficient with affricates, you would bounce back quickly and review some short vowels. *Word Journeys* has lists of words and phonics patterns for every stage in its appendix, and we listed some websites where you can find these in our resources section, too.

This is one way you can determine where to start the phonics part of your intervention. You could also start where you think most of the students you need to work with are based on assessments the school provides or your own formal or informal assessments. From there, you could follow one of the free scope and sequences noted in previous chapters or the scope and sequence your school is using in the primary grade foundational skills program. We know from David Paige's research that you need to get these students *at least* through the WWS and expose them to all of the phonics patterns in that stage before you can stop worrying about decoding and concentrate on just fluency.

The time you spend reteaching these phonics patterns is completely dependent upon your evaluation of your students' progress. It is likely your students will be all over the place in what they do and don't know (unless you're a parent with just your own child in mind or an intervention teacher in a position to group students by the results of their needs assessment). If so, you could also make use of peer coaching and buddy work to make things more manageable for you and perhaps more fun for the students. Let them teach each other what each partner already has mastered but her partner hasn't. Remember Gregory and Tyrone, back in chapter 5? That's what they started doing naturally. You're going to need to rely on your own evaluation of your student' needs to figure these questions of where to focus and how to group your students. Ideally, how fast your students move through the learning will determine the time you should give for each pattern.

No matter how you decide where to start and what your pace is, you'll approach the teaching of phonics patterns very differently with older students than with children learning foundational skills for the first time in the primary grades. That, too, may come as a "good news" story because as you'll see, everything we suggest is oriented to games and partner work. See for yourself! Here is how we recommend you go about this:

These are all activities that integrate the needed phonics exposures into your fluency work. Some focus more on reading words to achieve automaticity, others on spelling, some combine both. Remember these processes reinforce and strengthen each other. These activities can be done with any phonics pattern, can be repeated throughout the year, and are designed to move fast and be fun. They require few materials, although a bound notebook used only for this work would be helpful. How long you spend on any of these depends upon how well students are doing, how much they're enjoying the activity, and how much time you have to give it.

Let's start with an example of the different ways the /ā/ sound is spelled (/ai/ as in *paid*, /ay/ as in *bay*, /ei/ as in *sleigh*, a/C/e as in *make*, *lake*, etc.). Remember, however, these activities can be done with any phonics patterns. Show students examples of words with these patterns using the texts you just finished for fluency work or texts from previous weeks. Whenever possible, it's good to stick with texts students have read because this reinforces the learning. It also minimizes how much time you spend finding materials.

Working in pairs, have students find all the words in the passage containing any of these patterns and make a list. The list can be made either in a notebook students use for this time or sheets of paper, although the learning record a notebook offers is wonderful. If your students are used to working together in Google docs or other online tools, they could also store their learning and collaborate that way. Remember that these activities apply to work with any phonics patterns! We're just demonstrating using these digraphs.

Although the activities are straightforward and students will learn the routines quickly, you'll want to model when you introduce a new routine.

- Student-Led Dictations: After lists are finished, partners take turns dictating and spelling (without looking) the list to one another, one partner reading, the other spelling. Each partner should get at least two chances reading and spelling. Make it three "read-and-spells" if you think your students need more. If there are any words you think students won't know the meaning of, provide them up front. This is your basic starting activity with any phonics pattern. It gives students the opportunity to read, spell, and hear each word multiple times right at the outset. Remember, reading, hearing, and spelling all reinforce each other, making it more likely these word and the phonics pattern(s) the word holds will go into students' long-term memory and become automatic; you're making this more likely because of the repetitions. Unlike younger students in kindergarten through second grade learning to read for the first time, there's a limit to how much repetition older students who have been alienated from reading will tolerate. For that reason, "soup up" activities as much as you can and follow student leads when they get creative with the routines.

- Who's the Quickest?: Using a timer, have students race each other to see who reads the most words accurately from the list in 30 seconds (or reads all the words accurately in the fastest time). Students not reading should follow along as carefully as possible to see if any errors were made; if so, she should make the correction. If you have lots of timers or students are old enough to have phones, have them time each other as independent practice.
- Stop & Spot the Error!: While reading and spelling each word on the list, a student should randomly read or spell a word *deliberately* incorrectly to her partner. If her partner hears it, she says, "stop" and reads or spells it correctly.
- Name that Pattern: Taking turns, students read one word at a time to each other. This time, after reading a word, the student spells it and states the phonics pattern (here, what is making the /Ā/ sound). For example, for *claim*, the student reads, "Claim. c-l-a-i-m, the /ā/ sound is made by /ai/."
- Name Another Pattern: Same as above, but this time, students state another known phonics pattern that appears in each word. For example: "Framed. The /fr/ is made by the 'fr' consonant blend." The /Ā/ sound is made by the "aCe" (magic 'e') pattern.

Extension at Home (If Appropriate)

These can be done in addition to the fluency work at home.

- See if any of the adults or older siblings at home can read the list as fast as the student can.
- Give someone at home a spelling test using the words.

[3] Abstract vowels are vowels that make a sound other than a short or long sound. Examples are 'oo,' 'oi,' 'ou,' and 'aw.'

- Teach the words to a younger sibling or friend. If the student has a pet dog, sit it down and read and spell the words to it. You'll find most dogs pay attention! The student can also ask for her dog's help with the fluency packet.
- Word Scramble: Students take five words from the day's list and scramble the order of the letters in each. They then send the scrambled words from home in a text message to a preassigned partner. The partner, meanwhile, will do the same. See who can unscramble the five words first and send them back to their partner.
- *You* scramble five words and text them to all the students (or put them on the class website). Part of homework is to unscramble. Next day, pairs read and spell words to each other.
- Using any text, the student should find 10 words containing the /Ā/ sound using at least one example of each spelling pattern you're working with. The student should write these in her notebook and prepare to read them out loud to the class the next day. The teacher will time the student, so she should practice reading them at home with someone to listen.

Advanced Work: Abstract Vowels[3] and Vowel Teams

In these examples, use the following abstract vowels or vowel teams: /oo/ as in *boom*, /ou/ as in *found*. Unlike the work with /Ā/ where all the phonics patterns made the same sound, with these words we now have different letter patterns making different sounds. You can add 'oi' here as well if you think your students can work with three phonics patterns.

- Finding the Examples: As with the list game, have students in pairs find all examples of each of these patterns in their fluency text. As students find each word, they should be sure to say it and spell it aloud as they write it in their notebooks.
- Sorting the Words by Pattern: Students separate the original list into two lists by spelling pattern at least one time. The reason for the extra round would be there's a lot going on and some students may need more repetitions before they're comfortable.
- Peer-to-Peer Mini–Spelling Tests: One student takes the original list and reads words aloud one at a time while her partner spells the words. Essentially, this is a mini–spelling test. Both students then check the spelled words together. Switch roles when done. It would be good if the more confident student volunteered to go first.

- Who Made the Most Words?: You put a series of letters on the board, including the abstract vowel teams. Each pair of students has five minutes to make as many words as they can with each pattern using only the letters on the board. When the winner is announced, they have to read and spell each word to the class to claim the mantel of "winner." Students need to clear their desk of any notes, and you need to cover your word walls or any other potentially helpful posters. If you're using student recording notebooks, they need to be put away. Use scraps of paper or whiteboards for students to record the words they make. In this game, students need to construct words from memory, which means they're doing the hard work of spelling the patterns they've been studying from scratch—their first-class ticket to automaticity.
- The Funniest Sentence: Students write one sentence for each word on their list; the goal is to make these as humorous as possible (while staying clean). At the end of the week, each student picks what she thinks is her funniest sentence and reads it aloud. The group picks a winner. You could keep these weekly submissions to publish toward the end of the year and share with your hard-working students!
- Backward Sentence Read: This activity should *only* be done with texts students have read multiple times, studied, and answered questions about. It could be the text from the original fluency protocol or a text from another part of your curriculum. It should be on grade level and just a short section. Challenge your students to read it backward! Not letter by letter but word by word, so instead of, "He saw that he would be in trouble," students would read, "trouble in be would he that saw He." There are two significant benefits to this. In reading, the context supports students' word recognition. "He saw that he would be in . . ." supports the student *anticipating* and then recognizing "trouble." Reading backward, no such support exists. Students need to focus more on each word. By doing that, they're strengthening their working memory of phonics patterns. This is one of our ideas that sounds silly if not downright subversive, but students think it's really funny. Many students have noticed that reading like this makes them sound like the Jedi Warrior, Yoda!

We have given many of these activities a competitive element to add excitement and fun. There is research that this approach enhances memory (McGaugh, 2006). But if you'd like, you can easily convert them into a noncompetitive format. For example, in The Funniest Sentence, eliminate voting for a winner and just have students read and laugh!

We've designed this section and used this approach with these activities primarily thinking of a tier two intervention in small groups. But there's no reason these routines, games, and protocols couldn't be used as tier one instruction, as well. Meredith essentially did in her CTE teaching years because virtually all her students needed fluency work.

Just as these activities can be used for one phonics pattern at a time as modeled, they can and should be used for cumulative reviews with any patterns you've worked with.

One excellent variation to do this kind of review work is to put all of the phonics patterns studied within the review period on the board. Working in pairs, students make one column for each pattern and hunt through any of the texts you've worked with to find 10 examples for each phonics pattern and record them in the column. Or the class could work together to make one Google doc that holds the patterns.

One column at a time is then first read and spelled to a partner, and then places are switched so both students get the review and practice. Once this is done for all of the phonics patterns, partners can take turns reading each column to each other as fast as they can with the partner following along and listening for errors.

The activities we've included here just scratch the surface of the possible. The important idea is to keep this learning as fresh and fun as possible so students willingly engage in backfilling their unfinished learning around foundational skills and reading fluency. That way, they can move forward with their grade-level peers as powerful readers.

Wrap-Up

The recommendations contained in this chapter are based on the research cited throughout this and other chapters. But just as important, they are based on success in numerous urban, suburban, and rural classes from grades two through 12. One of the greatest obstacles to these students with unfinished literacy learning catching up with their peers is time. The more time you can find—before school, during school, after school, and at home—the greater the chances of catching up. The other, steeper obstacle is how discouraged students with unfinished learning generally are, which gets worse the older they are. This is part of our work, too: to believe in students' ability to learn and to hold that vision for them until they can see enough progress to claim their abilities as their own. Remember, these students have to get automaticity with words and reading fluency their peers may have had for years. We want to be clear about this; as sure as we are they can catch up, we are equally sure it will take their time and your commitment. The older the student, the more energy it will take and the more complicated it is. But it is doable as long as all parties have the will and inspiration to keep on striving.

Sources for Deeper Learning and Teaching

Tim Raskinski and the Ohio Literacy Alliance

Source of free passages and guidance for high school fluency screening

http://literacy.kent.edu/ohioliteracyalliance/fluency/fluency.htm

Also from Tim Raskinski, a new, excellent, all-in-one resource for reading fluency:

Rasinski, T., & Cheesman Smith, M. (2018). *The Megabook of Fluency.* New York: Scholastic (Winner of the 2019 Teachers' Choice Award for the classroom).

Some of the games and competitive routines we're sharing we got from Dr. Tim Rasinski. We owe a special thanks to Dr. Rasinski for everything he's taught us about the importance of fluency. His generosity as a researcher and a creator of practical supports for the hard work of teaching stands out in the literacy field. He is a champion of the right of children to read always. Dr. Rasinski's website is located at https://www.timrasinski.com/resources.html, and you can see from visiting it just how rooted and connected he is to the classroom and the real world. Dr. Rasinski was the very first literacy researcher we reached out to in our own learning journey. We soon learned the graciousness of his response was part and parcel of who he is. He is also responsible for introducing us to the powerful intellect and energy of Dr. David Paige.

Achieve the Core Fluency Packets for older students

https://achievethecore.org/page/2948/fluency-resources-for-grade-level-routines

Achieve the Core Foundational Skills Resources

https://achievethecore.org/category/1206/ela-literacy-foundational-skills

Two sites that discuss the elements of phonics essential to developing automaticity in decoding

This link takes you to a resource maintained by the literacy team in a small Virginia county. It offers a page of definitions for the "letter naming" phase of phonics, which preceded the "within word patterns" stage.

https://sites.google.com/a/apps.fluco.org/carysbrook-literacy-partners/word-study/letter-name-stage

This is a link to a supporting document for Words Their Way about "Within Word Patterns" buried deep within Pearson/ Prentice Hall's teacher resources archives

It provides straightforward definitions and examples alongside some useful teacher tips.

http://www.phschool.com/wtw/WTW_TG_WWP_over.pdf

Ganske, Kathy. *Word Journeys*, Second Edition, The Guilford Press, 2014

Developmental Reading Assessment (DRA) MSWord version posted online. Retrieved January 4, 2019.

https://rcps.info/common/pages/DisplayFile.aspx?itemId=1077525

Spelling City

A useful website for lists of words with different phonics patterns and grade-level word lists. There is a premium membership, but you can access some resources for free.

https://www.spellingcity.com

Works Consulted

Biemiller, A. (2009). *Words worth teaching: Closing the vocabulary gap*. Columbus, OH: McGraw-Hill SRA.

Chard, D. J., Vaughn, S., & Tyler, B.-J. (2002). A synthesis of research on effective interventions for building reading fluency with elementary students with learning disabilities. *Journal of Learning Disabilities, 35*(5), 386–406. http://dx.doi.org/10.1177/00222194020350050101

Daane, M. C. (2005). *The nation's report card: Fourth-grade students reading aloud: NAEP 2002 special study of oral reading*. Washington, DC: National Center for Education Statistics.

Fuchs, L. S., Fuchs, D., Hosp, M. K., & Jenkins, J. R. (2001). Oral reading fluency as an indicator of reading competence: a theoretical, empirical, and historical analysis. *Scientific Studies of Reading, 5*, 239–256. Retrieved from http://web.ebscohost.com.pluma.sjfc.edu

Hock, M. F., Brasseur, I. F., Deshler, D. D., Catts, H. W., Marquis, J. G., Mark, C. A., & Stribling, J. W. (2009). What is the reading component skill profile of adolescent struggling readers in urban schools? *Learning Disability Quarterly, 32*, 21–38.

Jenkins, J. R., Fuchs, L. S., van den Broek, P., Espin, C., & Deno, S. L. (2003). Sources of individual differences in reading comprehension and reading fluency. *Journal of Educational Psychology, 95*(4), 719–729. http://dx.doi.org/10.1037/0022-0663.95.4.719

McGaugh, J. L. (2006). Make mild moments memorable: Add a little arousal. *Trends in Cognitive Sciences*, *10*, 345–347.

Paige, D. D. (2006). Increasing fluency in disabled middle school readers: Repeated reading utilizing above grade level reading passages. *Reading Horizons*, *46*, 167–181.

Paige, D. D. (2011). 16 minutes of "eyes-on-text" can make a difference: Whole-class choral reading as an adolescent fluency strategy. *Reading Horizons*, *51*, 1–20.

Stahl, S. A., & Heubach, K. M. (2005). Fluency-oriented reading instruction. *Journal of Literacy Research*, *37*, 25–60.

Torgesen, J. K., & Hudson, R. F. (2006). Reading fluency: Critical issues for struggling readers. In S. J. Samuels & A. Farstrup (Eds.), *Reading fluency: The forgotten dimension of reading success* (pp. 130–158). Newark, DE: International Reading Association. Retrieved from https://pdfs.semanticscholar.org/35eb/002b92640d32f38ae49c4483c1806cf42942.pdf

Conclusion

One last story for now. Zach was an affable seven-year-old child enrolled in a Montessori-style elementary school in Yonkers, New York. It was the spring of 1990, near the zenith of the Whole Language movement. Zach's elementary school had grabbed onto Whole Language, and there was a lovely culture in his classroom of environmental print, lots of reading aloud, and free-choice explorations. He was deep into first grade and making no progress in reading or writing. The kicker to his parents was when they realized he couldn't even recognize his own name in print. They went into high gear to get him evaluated, and he was placed into a special-education setting where his significant learning gaps could be attended to.

That seven-year-old Zach was our child, being raised by his parents and step-parents—three teachers and an editor. All avid readers. This was devastating to us. At that point, we were all teaching in middle and high schools and knew not a thing about the science of reading and what the brain needs to do to learn to read in English.

We knew Zach didn't ever do quiet things like puzzles and drawing, that he always preferred adult conversation and *loved* being read to or watching all kinds of elaborate movies. He knew a lot about the world from all that and was really verbal. We knew he was smart. We also noticed he shunned any kind of visual or fine-motor work, never pretend-wrote, never asked anything about print. We had no clue he wasn't progressing through the reading processes we've described in this book or that he had such a significant learning disability he couldn't spot his own name in print.

The entire extended family on both sides chipped in and helped pay the hefty tuition to get Zach into the Windward School in White Plains, New York, a remarkable place led by the peerless Judith Hochman, who much later would go on to found the Writing Revolution based on the teaching methods that were so successful at Windward.[1]

Fast forward two years. Zach was now in the spring of third grade at Windward getting his second year of intensive structured phonics and writing

[1] The Writing Revolution has a website and now offers resources like those Zach got at Windward, as well as excellent teacher professional development courses around solid writing instruction: https://www.thewritingrevolution.org/.

remediation with highly trained teachers. Windward had a strict policy that parents shouldn't tutor their children so students wouldn't have to bare their areas of greatest weakness at home. We understood and respected that. Anyway, we trusted he was getting the help he needed, and reports were good. We didn't have a clear sense of where he was because we just didn't know much about foundational reading, what can go very wrong, and what it looks like when it's going well.

This is Meredith's story:

I was with the boys doing errands one weekend and had parked Zach and his brother in the toy and books section of a big box store while I grabbed what I needed nearby. When I came back to get them, Zach was sitting on the floor with a remainder copy of a Hardy Boys mystery book, *The House on the Cliff*, open in his hands. He asked if he could get it. We were tight with money in those days (remember that hefty tuition added to our normal living costs and child support on two teachers' salaries?), so I said, "only if you can read it," figuring that was a surefire way to get out of the extra expense. Zach flipped open the book and proceeded to fluently read a couple of paragraphs, the first time I'd ever heard him read. Heck, it was the first time I'd ever seen him voluntarily *hold* a book. I'd been a Hardy Boys fan myself, and that second book was one of my favorites. I remembered the characters and old-fashioned language well. These weren't third-grade books. We brought home all the Hardy Boys books the store had in their discounted book section that day.

Zach left Windward reading just fine and scoring at grade level at the end of that same year. He mainstreamed into fourth grade at his public school pretty seamlessly. We were all greatly relieved at his growth (not to mention not having to figure out how to pay the tuition anymore!), and forever grateful to Windward and Dr. Hochman, but it all seemed like a magical cure to us. We knew Zach had a significant learning disability and just figured Windward addressed that. We didn't know then what he had gotten in intensive doses were the sense-making experiences that every child needs to experience in some form or another to learn to read. While every child doesn't need the intense phonics work Zach did, a systematic phonics approach benefits every child. It gives everyone a sense of how language works. It moves children to independent reading of more complex books more quickly, and it makes everyone into good spellers. If we provide it to everyone, all children benefit.

Looking back, we can't help but wonder what would have been different if he'd gone through elementary school at a time and place that valued and taught systematic phonics. Would he have gotten what he needed on time and been okay? Maybe a member of the slowest reading group, definitely that child who needed lots of repetition and practice, but would he have been identified as in crisis and in need of two years at a full-day special-education private school? We wonder about that, knowing now exactly what Zach needed.

There are countless children with needs like Zach had. They're sitting in elementary classrooms all over the country. They probably don't all have three teachers and an editor as their squadron of parents (not that we helped much) or extended family willing to chip in to cover tuition at a top-notch school that could address their reading delays. We were fortunate and so was Zach.

Roll the calendar forward almost 30 years. We now know too much about how the brain processes text—about the science of reading—for children to be dependent on good fortune and luck for whether or not they learn to read well.

Here's what we know. You know it now, too.

Cognitive scientists and reading researchers know how the brain learns to read.

Here's Mark Seidenberg's take on this:

> Is there an area in cognitive science and cognitive neuroscience that has been more successful than the study of reading? Let's not underestimate the amount that has been learned. We, the community of scientists who study reading . . . understand the basic mechanisms that support skilled reading, [and] how reading skill is acquired.[2]

Yet for the most part, elementary teachers aren't being provided with this knowledge. Not in preservice, not in professional development workshops once they're in classrooms. Although there has been a flurry of popular press wondering why our children can't read during the six months we were working on this book, how our children learn to read remains mysterious for many parents, too. David and I weren't all that unusual in not being on top of Zach's reading issues.

We wrote this book to address that knowledge gap—to explain as clearly and simply as we could what we've learned about reading. That way, teachers and parents can select a good reading program that makes sure children have the materials they need to do the systematic work and all the mix of rich language activities that will allow every child to enter the magical world of reading.

There are other reasons we wrote this book. With all our hearts, we believe in what we've tagged "Both/And." We believe in reading aloud and in systematic phonics. We believe in fun and play, all through the day. But we also know children need time for regular practice to gain new skills solidly. Some only need a little practice, and some, like Zach, far more. Most children fall somewhere in between. We're equally convinced children, in fact, like to be challenged intellectually. We believe in small-group and individual instruction, but we also believe that sometimes working with the whole class is both good

[2] Seidenberg M. S. (2013). The science of reading and its educational implications. *Language Learning and Development: The Official Journal of the Society for Language Development*, 9, 331–360.

for everybody *and* more efficient. We believe teaching is an art—but an art based on science.

We wrote this book because the cost of not teaching so many children to read is unacceptable. The heavy cost is borne disproportionately by children who are raised in poverty, students who already know another language but need to learn English too, and the growing numbers of American children of color.

We are at our core teachers, with 48 classroom years between us. We know turning around literacy outcomes for our nation's children is completely achievable. But we also know this fix takes time, heart, and work from teachers. Most of all, we know *nothing* works in education unless teachers believe in it and understand it. We hope we've helped with that.

Thanks for your care and attention.
David and Meredith Liben

We want to hear your stories and any wonderings, questions, better resources, or points of disagreements you may have. Our website is Reading Done Right (www.readingdoneright.org), and there's a section dedicated to this book, a resources and essential readings section, and ways for you to contact us. Please do!

"When you learn, teach. When you get, give."
–Maya Angelou

Programs We Recommend

These five core English Language Arts (ELA) programs all incorporate a strong systematic phonics program for kindergarten through second grade with excellent core ELA approaches. Although they all have systematic, research-based foundational skills programs, they are very different from each other in a number of ways. In each case, we'll briefly describe the program with an emphasis on how it differs from the others, say what we see as its strong elements, point out what you might want to adjust for, and highlight what to consider regarding whether it could be a good fit for your school or district. Any of these programs that have been reviewed by the independent program evaluation group Ed Reports[1] has received "all greens" (high marks) for foundational skills. We'll also tell you how you can find more information directly from the developers of each program.

Although all these programs include phonemic awareness, we don't feel any of them give it enough of an emphasis (we have high standards!). This problem can be solved by supplementing with Marilyn Adam's *Phonemic Awareness in Young Children,* which we discussed in chapter three. It's an inexpensive solution because you only need one book per teacher.

Finally, although all of these programs are full ELA programs that exist for various grade spans from pre-K through 12th grade, we're addressing only the foundational skills component of each program. You can find out more about the full programs from the developers, on Ed Reports, or on the *Aligned* blog on Achieve the Core.

The programs are discussed in reverse alphabetical order for no other reasons than to be fair and quirky.

Wit and Wisdom from Great Minds

Wit and Wisdom is a core ELA program from Great Minds, the not-for-profit company that developed Eureka Math. As with the others, its foundational skills program has everything we've discussed as being necessary.

[1] For more information about Ed Reports, including access to the full reports on these programs, go to https://www.edreports.org/ela/reports/index.html.

Great Minds contracted with Wilson Language Training to license "Fundations," a stand-alone systematic phonics program, for *Wit and Wisdom*. Fundations never developed any decodable readers, so the *Wit and Wisdom* team made their own decodables, which they've named Geodes, after the spherical rocks that yield beautiful crystals when they're broken open. These are like no decodable ever made and, in many respects, are unique in young children's literature. The Geodes are beautifully crafted both in illustrations and words. In addition, all the decodables are connected to the topics studied in the accompanying ELA units, so children reading Geodes get to build knowledge and read meaningful text while they're practicing their phonics in context. In addition to the content and phonics patterns, each Geode includes vocabulary words, phonemic awareness activities, an array of good questions, and suggestions for further learning.

The Geodes and *Wit and Wisdom*, in general, integrate art and art history lessons into the curriculum more than any other ELA program. If you purchase Fundations with the Geodes, you'll have an excellent free-standing foundational skills program, but you'll lose the lovely integration with the *Wit and Wisdom* ELA content.

Wit and Wisdom for kindergarten through second grade hasn't yet been reviewed by Ed Reports as of this writing, but the reports will be available by the time you're reading this. The program for grades three through eight received all greens from Ed Reports.

Samples and more information are available at Great Minds Geodes (https://gm.greatminds.org/geodes-readable-library) or Wit and Wisdom (https://greatminds.org/english) for information on the full ELA program, and at Wilson for the matching Fundations program (https://www.wilsonlanguage.com/programs/fundations/).

EL Education

The EL skills program, as is true of all of these, is part of a full core ELA program. It can *easily* be used separately from the larger core program. EL was developed as an open educational resource (OER), which means the skills program and decodables (and all the ELA lessons) can be downloaded and used for free from EL Education's website (https://curriculum.eleducation.org/curriculum/search). That will work if you're very organized and have access to reams of paper! The materials are also distributed through Open Up Resources (OUR; https://openupresources.org/el-education-k-5-language-arts/) in a bound and organized printed form for purchase, which we'd recommend if you're using the full skills program rather than using it to supplement your own materials. The EL skills component adheres to everything we have discussed in this book.

EL Education pulled out all the stops to make learning phonics a joyful and invigorating experience. It's almost as if a Broadway Musical were the model for the vibrant lessons. It makes learning how to read lively to a degree no other program matches. Many teachers have gotten back to us confirming that.

Integral to EL's philosophy is the goal of helping students take charge of their own learning. This means that embedded in every foundational skills lesson will be moments when students evaluate their progress and take stock of what they're learning about the English language.

The decodables for EL are minimalist, meaning the language is very simple. The decodable readers are small booklets, nowhere near as elaborate as the Geodes. What EL has done that's lovely is they've carefully aligned their decodables with a richer, more complex read-aloud story, thus making them far more engaging. Early on in the kindergarten read-aloud, the stories are crafted to engage students in learning about how letters and sounds work together. Children love these stories.

EL Education for kindergarten through fifth grade has been reviewed by Ed Reports and received all greens.

Core Knowledge Language Arts

Core Knowledge Language Arts (CKLA) is the other foundational skills program discussed here that, like EL Education, is *completely* self-contained and available free for the printing as an OER. Called the "Skills Strand," it's half the ELA program. The other part is called "Listening and Learning."

The Skills Strand of the CKLA is one of the few newer foundational skills programs that has been evaluated over a three-year period in a major research project. Ten schools were trained in using CKLA and used it schoolwide. Ten control schools kept on using their existing program, which was the popular Balanced Literacy program, Teachers College Reading and Writing Project (TCRWP). After three years, results on a variety of national standardized foundational skills tests were compared.[2] The schools using CKLA outperformed the schools using TCRWP in every test. Research projects with 10 schools over a three-year period are extremely rare, and this was an important finding.

CKLA has all the elements of systematic phonics that we've described as essential. One outstanding feature of the program is how they've developed the decodable texts. These texts are highly decodable but also *far* more interesting than traditional decodables. They are all stories, but these are

[2] See the full report here: https://www.coreknowledge.org/wp-content/uploads/2016/12/CK-Early-Literacy-Pilot-3-12-121.pdf.

stories about children who find ancient coins and learn about them with coin collectors; Mexican American families visiting grandparents in Mexico; grandmothers who learn how to hang glide, etc. Many of the stories follow the same family, so children feel they're reading "chapter books" and are very proud of themselves. Interestingly, we've noticed that boys especially find these stories especially appealing.

CKLA introduces letter sounds before letter names, which is unusual. The names are introduced quickly, but we've found this throws off some teachers, so we wanted to mention it. The idea is that letter sounds are what are used to read words, not their names. As we noted in chapter 1, letter names are useful as labels, and they're useful in terms of communicating about what we're busy studying. It's useful to know the letter names when you're working with them.

There's no research showing that the CKLA approach is harmful, so we recommend that teachers either follow the program as is (if they're comfortable with this approach) or just ignore it and teach the letter names along with the sounds if they aren't.

As we discussed in chapter 5, CKLA has something called the "Assessment and Remediation Guide." This is a compilation of activities, games, and lessons for every phonics pattern for assessing and reteaching and can be downloaded for free with or without the rest of the program.

The CKLA skills program is available in all its forms here, at the Core Knowledge Foundation (https://www.coreknowledge.org/curriculum/download-curriculum/). You can choose to download, print, and organize everything for free, but the same caveat applies as with EL Education. The complete skills component can be purchased from Amplify (https://www.amplify.com/programs/amplify-core-knowledge-language-arts/) complete with all the supports. When done this way, the decodables come as bound books. If possible, we strongly recommend purchasing the program because the materials are beautiful when commercially published, and children really enjoy holding and reading books. You can link to the Amplify commercial version from the Foundation's website (https://www.coreknowledge.org/curriculum/language-arts/).

CKLA, too, received all greens on Ed Reports.

Bookworms

Bookworms was developed by two reading researchers and is completely research based. It is the newest and most streamlined of these comprehensive programs and integrates all of what we've described as essential in their foundational skills program. It, too, is an open educational resource, but it's built entirely around trade books that have to be purchased. Unlike any of these other programs, the *Bookworms* foundational skills program cannot be purchased separately from the full core ELA program. This is because, rather than using stand-alone decodable readers, *Bookworms* provides brief decodable readings for the phonics patterns students are learning and then reinforces the patterns systematically in the full-length trade literature it uses for shared reading in its comprehension program.

Bookworms is an excellent, easy-to-implement program. Like *Wit and Wisdom*, the expanded second version has not been reviewed completely by Ed Reports as of this writing. Bookworms is distributed by Open Up Resources and information and samples can be found at OUR (https://openupresources.org/bookworms-k-5-reading-writing-curriculum/).

American Reading Company

American Reading Company (ARC) was founded in 1997 by a reading specialist but only recently developed its ARC Core Program. It is the only kindergarten through 12th-grade program reviewed and given all green on Ed Reports.

ARC Core has all the elements of systematic phonics and solid foundational skills work we've emphasized. But it's an *analytic* phonics program and not a *synthetic* phonics program as all these other programs are. Analytic phonics works by analogy, or a focus on onsets and rimes, rather than an emphasis on phonemes. For example, the word *look* might be taught as a sight word and used to teach *book*, *took*, *hook*, *foot*, *hoof*, *good*, etc. So it is a different approach. The National Reading Panel was very clear that as long as programs and instruction are systematic, results for groups of children were equal. In our experience, analytic phonics, at least as taught in ARC, is significantly easier for teachers to learn than most synthetic programs. Synthetic programs, however, provide a greater insight into the workings of the language than the analytic approach.

ARC's foundational skills program can easily be purchased separately, and several schools we know have done that and been very happy with the results.

Instead of decodable readers, ARC uses trade literature for reading the patterns and sight words students learn after roughly the kindergarten level of their Independent Reading Level Assessment, or IRLA, that the program is designed around. We have found these books quite engaging, which makes the multiple readings necessary for many students more fun and engaging. ARC also includes many riddles, games, and fun activities as part of its foundational skills program.

Information for ARC Core (https://www.americanreading.com/documents/arc-core-overview.pdf) or IRLA (https://www.americanreading.com/leveling/overview/) can also be found at the main portal, https://www.americanreading.com/. ARC Core also exists as a Spanish-language program in its entirety, the only one of these programs this is true for.

CPSIA information can be obtained
at www.ICGtesting.com
Printed in the USA
BVHW011512070721
611371BV00002B/4